HOW TO *EASILY* MANAGE YOUR RENTAL PROPERTY IN
ENGLAND

HOW TO *EASILY* MANAGE YOUR RENTAL PROPERTY IN ENGLAND

Meet the necessary legal requirements and test your knowledge of renting a property in England

Marie Lamb

Disclaimer

The information in this book has been carefully put together using law reference materials and research but its accuracy cannot be guaranteed as laws in respect of landlords and tenants are subject to regular updates and changes. This book incorporates the recent changes to legislation as of July 2018.

For information visit http://learn2let.co.uk

The author will not accept responsibility for any loss or damage alleged to be caused by information contained/not contained in this book.

Please note: this book will help you understand the law in the area where you are renting out a property but it is not a substitute for advice from a solicitor. If in doubt you should always seek professional advice.

First Edition
ISBN: 978-1-9999617-0-1

Foreword

Being a landlord is big responsibility and there are many procedures to consider before handing over the keys to someone else. If a landlord employs a letting agent, essentially the landlord is authorising the agent to act on their behalf. If the agent is acting in a wrongful manner from a legal point of view, the landlord will also be held responsible.

Landlords can avoid the most common legal mistakes by learning the fundamental steps to managing their rental property. Most investors would not start a business without at least some awareness of the legal steps involved. Investing in property is no different. A simple mistake can prove to be a living nightmare for landlords. And....simple mistakes can be made quite easily. As they say, knowledge is power, the more you know the more confident you will feel should anything go wrong!

England, Wales and Scotland have very different legal rules when it comes to renting a property. This book has been produced to give the landlord clear and concise guidelines relating to the law and obligations in the area where they are renting out their property.

So... whether you are a landlord employing a letting agent, or managing the property yourself, knowing your rights and responsibilities is the first step in protecting you, your tenant and your property!

This book has up-to-date legal information and sample forms. It relates specifically to property rentals in England. The book comprises six sections and at the end of each section, recap questions will consolidate the lessons learnt. Self-check questions are included at the end of the book.

About the Author

My name is Marie Lamb. I am a Tutor/Trainer. Over the last fifteen years I have taught many landlords how to manage their rental property or properties. I have the (ARLA) Association of Residential Letting Agencies technical qualification and am passionate about all things property.

When I hear horror stories about how tenants have abused properties, I have to wonder – is it down to bad luck or is it the landlord not taking more of an active interest? Put it like this, if you returned an item to a shop and the assistant wasn't very helpful - you would ask to see the manager right? If the manager wasn't available and the assistant was unhelpful, you would start to get frustrated and annoyed and get the impression that you are not being taken seriously - basically this is what can happen to your tenants.

Of the many landlords who have attended my workshops, the self-managed ones are the ones who rarely have problems with their tenants. Obvious proof that having a good relationship with your tenant and knowing what you are doing is key to a smooth running rental.

Of course you don't have to manage your property yourself but if you don't know the first thing about letting your property how do you know if the agent is doing the job properly? It's in your interest to brush up on the law, know what needs to be done and keep on top of it.

CONTENTS

SECTION 3: RESPONSIBILITIES AND LIABILITIES

SECTION 4: DURING A TENANCY

SECTION 5: ENDING A TENANCY

SECTION 6: FORMS

SECTION 1

General Overview

Tenant Guide – How to Rent

The government tenant guide has been produced to help tenants understand what is involved when renting a property. Many problems have arisen in the past due to a tenant's lack of knowledge. To make the process a little easier for both landlords and tenants the government has produced a guide and made it compulsory for all landlords to give a copy to their tenant(s). The guide explains where tenants can get help and advice and what to do if things go wrong.

The tenant guide can be downloaded from the government website https://www.gov.uk/government/publications/how-to-rent. You can send a link to the tenant(s) but it is more advisable to issue them with a hard copy and keep a record of their signature stating that they have received it.

Note: Check the above website for the latest changes to the tenant guide. If you are not aware of any changes you could be giving your tenant(s) an out of date copy. It is therefore important to ensure that what you give any new tenant(s) is the most up-to-date version. Failure to follow this procedure could cause you problems at the end of the tenancy when trying to gain the property back.

I cannot stress enough the importance of maintaining records and keeping copies of any documents you issue to the tenants, and wherever possible, always ask the tenant(s) to sign a copy. You never know when you may have to rely on these documents and signatures!

Buy-to-Let

Investing in property can be a very lucrative business. The Buy-to-Let (BTL) industry can be more profitable than many other types of investments. Many people have bought property as a long-term investment instead of saving funds for a pension. It makes sense to have an investment that brings in a monthly income whilst the investment itself is still growing in value. If you are buying a property to let then you will require a BTL mortgage. These mortgages aren't subject to the same conditions as regular ones; they are generally based on the predicted rental income, rather than the buyer's income or means.

Not everyone chooses to buy property; some people inherit a property (referred to as accidental landlords) and some may keep a previous home when they upgrade to another. There are many reasons for landlords to acquire a BTL. You could be a professional landlord having ownership of several properties, or a landlord owning only one property.

Rental Yield

Most property investors will calculate their return on investment (ROI) using the formula below. This is called the rental yield. The rental yield is the amount of money a landlord receives in rent over a year, shown as a percentage of the amount of money invested in the property.

This is how to calculate the rental yield:

The Formula:
A BTL is purchased for £250,000 and rent is £800 per month;

800 x 12 (Annual rent) = 9600
£9,600/£250,000 = 0.0384 annual rent divided by the investment
0.0384*100 = 3.84% yield
The higher the yield, the better the investment.

Although, in reality, this is the yield only if you are buying the property outright. The actual return will be different if you take into account the money you borrow (if you require a mortgage) and also other costs when buying a property, such as stamp duty and legal fees, etc.

A property investor will also have to take into account costs related with renting the property, such as maintenance, repairs, insurance, letting management fees and so on. These costs have to be factored in when calculating the return on investment (ROI).

So how do landlords make a profit? Most make their money in two main ways: rent and selling. The capital growth from selling a property, for most landlords, will be the main aspect. After all, few landlords make a loss on their investment when selling properties.

Agent – Landlord Relationship

For legal purposes an agent is sometimes referred to as a 'Letting Negotiator' or a 'Management Agent', but is mostly referred to as a 'Letting Agent': a person who has the power to represent another legal party (the principal). The letting agent brings the principal (the landlord) into a legal relationship with a third party. In the case of letting agents and landlords the letting agent is the person who represents the landlord. Therefore, the landlord is the principal and the tenant is the third party.

If an agent fails to pay a third party or if an agent disappears with any money paid by a third party, the principal remains liable.

It is important to note that if landlords employ an agent to manage their property they still have a legal responsibility. Landlords cannot hide behind their lack of knowledge or ignorance in respect of the housing law. If an agent does anything wrong, from a legal point of view the landlord will also be held responsible.

How is an agency relationship created?

This may be created by a formal written contract, but sometimes can be (in law) implied by the conduct of the parties.

Agent's Main Duties to his Principal:

- ✓ To follow instructions
- ✓ To exercise due care and skill
- ✓ To carry out instructions
- ✓ To keep account of money owed
- ✓ Not to allow a conflict of interest

✓ Not to make a secret profit
✓ Not to take a bribe

The Agent's Legal Rights:

✓ To claim payment for services performed
✓ To claim expenses legitimately incurred
✓ To exercise a lien (retain and hold goods pending payment) over the principal's property

Note: Liens on property is a common way for creditors to collect what they are owed.

Agent's Fees

New laws are now in force (from June 1 2019) banning agents or Landlords from charging any kind of administration fees to the tenant. If Agents take a holding deposit they will only be allowed to take equivalent to one weeks' rent. Furthermore, they will not be allowed to advertise the property once they have the tenants holding fee. The fee will have to be repaid once the tenant has signed the agreement or 15 days if the agreement doesn't go ahead. Deposits are now capped at five weeks for annual rents under £50,000.

Note: You will still be able to charge tenants for things such as; replacement keys (providing you can show a receipt for getting a new key cut). You will also be able to charge reasonable cost for changing a tenancy agreement.

If you are unsure of the charges you can pass to the tenant you would be well advised to check the new legislation either on the government website or one of the landlords associations.

Common Law and Statute

Legislation or statute law has become the dominant form of law. They are those laws contained in Acts of Parliament. This basically means that the courts must apply the laws that have been passed.

Common law is effectively all law that has not been enacted by Parliament. It goes back hundreds of years and is formed from local custom which has now become common law. This basically means that a judge would have to use these customs to assess a court hearing using his/her experience, knowledge and judgement in the books of ancient law.

Organisations

Redress Scheme

If a letting agent belongs to an organisation such as ARLA Propertymark, RLA, NALS or RICS, this means the agency has agreed to meet the standards of the organisation it belongs to. This generally means they will offer a 'Client Money Protection Scheme' and have a customer complaints procedure, offering independent redress. In essence, if landlords make a complaint about any of the services they receive from their letting agent, the redress scheme will investigate the issue.

Client Money Protection (CMP)

From 27 May 2015, under the requirements set out in the 'Consumer Rights Act', it became compulsory for all agents to display in their offices and on their websites whether or not they are part of a 'Client Money Protection Scheme'. Client Money means money of any currency (whether in the form of cash, cheque, draft or electronic transfer).

One of the schemes is the 'Safe Agent' scheme, which offers consumers financial protection as well as peace of mind for landlords and tenants knowing that their money is protected through a CMP scheme. The scheme shows best practice, in particular in holding a client's money separately from the agent's money. Letting agents hold many thousands of pounds of both tenant and landlord money such as: holding deposits, dilapidation deposits etc. before the money is placed in a deposit scheme.

The Safe Agent scheme ensures the tenant's money is protected at all times. If an agent becomes a member of the Safe Agent scheme they will be given a sticker to display in their premises to comply with consumer regulations. Always check that an agent is a member of one of the CMP schemes!

A Letting Agent's Terms of Business

If an agent offers a full management service they may deal with all management issues - repairs, rent collection, starting the tenancy and advice on ending a tenancy.

It is the landlord's responsibility to keep on top of repairs and make sure they are undertaken as soon as possible. However, If an agent is appointed to act on a landlord's behalf to deal with repairs it is important that both the agent and landlord establish exactly what the agent is authorised to do. The agent needs to clarify with the landlord what repairs can be done without asking the landlord's consent. This is usually set out in the agency terms.

It is paramount that a landlord understands the extent of the agent's role. For example, a landlord must allow the agent to manage the property on his or her behalf and not put limitations or restrictions on the agent that make it impossible for the agent to fulfil his role. A landlord must not expect the agent to carry out duties beyond those that are stated in the agent's terms of business.

If for example, a landlord instructs an agent to perform tasks that are outside the agent's terms and conditions or are deemed illegal, the agent should remind the landlord of his/ her legal and contractual obligations. Most letting agencies will have provisions in their terms and conditions to terminate their contract with the landlord if they refuse to follow any of the Housing Act's legal requirements.

The Agent's Duties

A lettings agent's business is to find tenants and manage their clients' (the landlord's) investments in line with the landlord's instructions and this could include;

- Advising landlords about the letting procedures and market rent
- Arranging for maintenance/repairs to be carried out (if agreed in the agent's terms and conditions)
- Ensure that (if requested) they pay the premium for the renewal of the Landlord's insurance
- Setting up viewings and showing potential tenants around the property
- Selecting responsible, reliable tenants and preparing tenancy contracts and inventories (in most cases the agency will outsource the inventory)
- Checking tenant references ensuring all aspects of the letting meet the legal requirements
- Working with a wide range of people, such as solicitors, builders, cleaners and suppliers
- Handling any problems with the property (according to their terms and conditions)
- Keeping themselves and the landlord up-to-date with any changes in the housing law

Letting Options

Management Agent Services

Most management agencies offer three types of services.

This is an example of services provided by a letting agent:

Tenant Find Only

- ✓ Advertising for a tenant
- ✓ Viewings
- ✓ Tenant's reference and credit checks
- ✓ Setting up the tenancy contracts

Tenant Find and Rent Collection

The agent finds the tenants, takes up references and arranges the regular collection of rent. The fee is usually the same as for 'tenant find only', plus a percentage of the rental income.

Full Management

- ✓ Advertising for a tenant
- ✓ Viewings
- ✓ Tenant's referencing and credit checks
- ✓ Setting up the tenancy contracts
- ✓ Arranging gas and electricity certificates
- ✓ Meter readings and informing appropriate utilities
- ✓ Inventory and schedule of condition of the property

✓ Collection of rent and payment into the landlord's bank account
✓ Regular Inspections of property
✓ Day-to-day management and dealing with emergency issues relating to the property - subject to what has been discussed with the landlord

The 'Tenant Find Only' and 'Tenant Find and Rent Collection' options allow landlords the flexibility to manage the property themselves.

Additional Agent Services

Letting agents may offer additional services, for example: a landlord can arrange with the agent to perform essential work in preparation for letting a property. The agreement with the agent could cover charges, the amount of work involved and how the landlord will pay for the service if the agent has been instructed to pay contractors.

If a property is empty for a period of time, the landlord's insurance may become invalid. The landlord could arrange to pay an agent to visit the property regularly to check the security of the property and/or check for signs of damage or any repairs required.

Mortgages

Home owners will need to have a Buy-to-Let (BTL) mortgage before they can let their property. They need to inform their lender and obtain their permission. It is important that they get permission in writing from the mortgage lender, their insurer and their landlord (if they have a leasehold property) before they let their property to tenants. There are serious consequences if a home owner does not comply with the rules and conditions set out by their mortgage provider, for example, insurance cover could become void. If the property is a leasehold property (see next page) they will need to look closely at the clauses and in particular the head lease.

When a buyer signs a mortgage contract, the terms and conditions almost certainly state that if they wanted to let the property, they must seek permission. They will also be expected to pay a higher interest fee. If they break the mortgage agreement, and the lender finds out, then they can and will be in serious trouble. The lender may make the home owner pay the 'consent-to-let fee' at a higher rate, call in the debt or put a black mark against the home owner's name causing them future problems with their credit rating.

It is important to understand that letting a property with normal residential home insurance will almost certainly invalidate the insurance and this could prove expensive, for example, if there is a fire at the property. Landlords require specific landlord insurance policies and if they don't have permission from their lender then it is more than likely that no insurance company will insure their property. If a home owner is renting under a long lease, the property will be subject to the terms of the lease. It is very common for a freeholder to include a provision requiring the owner to gain permission before sub-letting a property. In some cases, if more than a third of the individual flats in a block are sub-let, the freeholder will need to apply for a Housing in Multiple Occupation (HMO) Licence (more about HMO's later). For this reason it is important to let the freeholder know of any intention to let the property.

Leasehold and Freehold

Definition of a Lease

A lease is a legal document detailing the terms under which one party agrees to rent property from another party. A lease guarantees the lessee (the renter) use of an asset and guarantees the lessor (the property owner) regular payments from the lessee for a specified number of months or years. This is sometimes referred to as 'Ground Rent'. Both the lessee and the lessor must uphold the terms of the contract for the lease to remain valid.

Note: the term rental agreement is also sometimes used to describe a periodic lease agreement (most often a month-to-month lease).

Flats/apartments are most commonly owned on a leasehold basis, while houses are normally owned as freehold properties.

If you buy a leasehold property you'll be known as the 'Leaseholder'. This means you own the property but not the land it stands on. Buying a freehold property means that you're the sole owner of both the building and the land it stands on.

If you own a home on a freehold basis, it is part of your estate and can be passed on to your heirs when you die.

With leasehold properties the land remains owned by the landlord, who is also known as the 'Freeholder'. Ownership of the property will revert back to them once the lease runs out. Leaseholders have to obtain permission from the freeholder to sub-let a leasehold property. It is also normal for the leaseholder to pay an annual fee to a managing agent.

Note: A management agent (in the case of leasehold) is someone who looks after the communal areas and the day-to-day running of the property.

Overseas Landlords

Often landlords decide to move abroad and use the proceeds from their rental property to fund a different way of life. However, there are legal considerations to take into account. If a landlord spends six months out of the country in any tax year, he/she will be classed as an overseas landlord. They must apply to the centre for non-residents (CNR) through HM Revenue & Customs for consent for the gross rental income to be passed onto them. Form NRL1 (Non Resident Landlord) for individual Landlords, NRL2 if the landlord is an offshore company or form NRL3 if the landlord is an offshore trust.

If a landlord does not have an approved number the responsibility will fall to the tenant to deduct tax. The landlord or agent should submit the relevant NRL form to the CNR. Once the form is received by the Inland Revenue, they will provide the tenant with an approved number.

Note: All new tenants will have to have a new approved number.

If a landlord is unsure about tax for overseas landlords, they should obtain further information from CNR which is based in Bootle Merseyside.

Insurances

A letting agent cannot make or process an insurance claim for the landlord unless they are authorised to do so. If the agent is authorised, he must, when dealing with repairs, follow the instructions of the insurance company or the loss adjuster. Insurance companies generally have their own preferred contractors to carry out work. Problems could arise if the agent instructs someone else to do the work before being authorised to do so. The agent must also be aware that a delay in making a claim may invalidate the insurance.

Insurances include: Building, Contents, Public Liability, Rent Guarantee, and Legal Expenses.

The following is an outline of some insurance policies a landlord may require:

Public Liability

Public Liability insurance covers any award or damages caused to a member of the public should they have an accident that resulted in an injury at your property. It can also cover legal fees and expenses associated with injury at a property. Premiums vary depending on the circumstances. There are many conditions that can be applied to public liability policies. It is therefore important that a landlord discusses their details with their Insurance broker. If a landlord chooses to deal directly with an insurer it is worthwhile checking that they are a member of the Association of British Insurers (ABI).

Landlords may think they don't need Public Liability Insurance; however, they may be wrong! Usually buildings policies will provide some kind of 'Employers' Liability' cover but they may not be covered if for example they employ any tradesmen at their property such as a gardener or decorator.

Buildings Insurance

In the case of residential property it is the landlord's responsibility to insure the building and its contents, but this does not include the tenants' contents nor does it include accidental damage to the landlord's property caused by the tenants. The tenants usually pay a security deposit (detailed later) at the beginning of the tenancy which should cover certain damages.

It is advisable for landlords to insure their buildings against all insurable risks to the full replacement cost. It is also important to include the cost of clearing the site after complete destruction. The replacement cost is not necessarily the same as the market value of the property or the price paid for it. By calculating the replacement value accurately you will be saving yourself time, money and heartache should anything untoward happen. A reasonably accurate insurance valuation on standard types of residential property can be obtained from the Association of British Insurers (ABI) website using their Building Costs Calculator.

In the case of unusual properties such as old, listed, conservation area, thatched or other specialist properties, it is worth obtaining a professional insurance valuation by a Chartered Building Surveyor. Most popular building risk policies include: Burglary and Theft, Bursts and Water leaks, Fire, Smoke, Storm and Flood, Subsidence, Vehicle Impact, Aircraft Damage, Lightening, Explosion and Malicious Damage. It is important to read the small print of any insurance policy to check that coverage is adequate.

Loss of Rent

Most specialist landlord policies will cover loss of rent and tenant accommodation cover, in the event of a major incident where the building is rendered uninhabitable. Some insurers have excess charges that can make the policy appear very competitive on price, so compare policies carefully before choosing.

Contents Insurance

If the tenant is responsible for most of the contents within the property, landlords do not normally need full contents cover. However, if the property is let on a fully furnished basis it may be more appropriate to insure for full contents cover. All furniture will need to meet the standard requirements (see later).

Many tenants don't give much thought to insurance with all the other expenses involved with renting a property. It's not going to be high on their list of priorities. And, most tenants in today's world own expensive equipment, cameras and laptops for example. It is well worth encouraging tenants to insure their contents against theft and burglary.

Rent Guarantee Insurance

If the landlord has carried out the tenant reference checking in the correct way, hopefully the tenants will be able to meet the rent. However, even performing thorough checks does not mean tenants will never experience difficulties in paying the rent. Despite the best will in the world, things can happen. Tenants can suddenly fall ill or their job may be made redundant. If a landlord is unlucky enough to find their tenant in any of these situations they could be in for a long battle of trying to obtain rent arrears and gaining their property back.

Rent Guarantee Insurance is an excellent and cost-effective way to minimise risks and is especially valuable for landlords. Charges may be as little as 3% of the rental value of the property and this option is well worth exploring with an Insurance Broker.

Note: For obvious reasons 'Rent Guarantee Insurance' is only obtainable once comprehensive references and credit checks have been obtained.

Legal Expenses Insurance

As mentioned earlier, the careful screening of tenants is the key to getting it right and nine times out of ten things will run smoothly, but occasionally through no fault of the tenant, things can start to go downhill. Certain situations cannot be avoided but, whatever the reason, the landlord could find himself with a legal battle on his hands! Proceedings to gain the property back could take months and costs can quickly get out of hand. A small annual sum spent on landlord's legal expenses insurance can help cover this eventuality. It's definitely worth looking into!

Tax

The dreaded subject of tax is something we all hate to talk about. However, knowing what your commitments are and being organised is vital to the smooth running of your business. The good news is that there are a number of expenses that can be offset against tax. Deductible expenses are classed as money a landlord spends on the day-to-day running of the property, such as reasonable management fees, accounting fees and so on. However, a landlord cannot claim fees for managing the property themselves. These only apply if the landlord employs a letting agent. Planning is essential and can make a difference to your overall returns, but tax is a complicated area and expert advice should be always be sought.

Section 24

Landlords should also be aware that in the Summer Budget (2015) it was announced that from April 2017, landlords would no longer be able to claim tax relief worth 40% or 45% on the interest payments on their buy-to-let mortgages. Instead, the maximum tax relief will be set at 20%, although these changes are said to be introduced over a four-year period. This section 24 legislation will inevitability restrict how much landlords can offset mortgage interest costs against profit.

If a landlord is not already aware of this new proposal, they would be well advised to read the information on the government website.

Keeping Tax Records

It is important that landlords keep records of receipts and any tax-deductible items for, up to six years after the tax year to which they apply – whether they complete a tax return or not!

Council Tax

When a property is let, it is important that the local authorities are notified of the following information:

- The name(s) of the tenant(s)
- Start date of the tenancy
- Tenancy duration

If a tenant vacates a property during a tenancy, they may still be liable for council tax, depending on the terms of the tenancy contract. Unless of course the property is re-let prior to expiry of the tenancy.

Properties let to Students

Full-time students are usually exempt for council tax purposes, but the authorities will still need proof that they are students. It is important that the landlord informs the authorities of the following:

- Student names
- Date the tenancy commenced
- Duration of the tenancy

The authorities will then contact the individuals and check their status. This usually applies to 'Houses in Multiple Occupation' (HMOs). (More about HMOs later)

Responsibilities of Students and Landlords

It is the responsibility of the liable person(s) to provide evidence of student status. If the students are liable, they should contact the authorities and let them know the course they are attending. They will then be told whether or not a student certificate needs to be provided.

If you are unsure about council tax discounts you would be well advised to brush up your knowledge on the government website.

Planning Permission and Building Regulations

No one is allowed to start development of land or property without permission from the local planning authority. The owner of the property (or land) is ultimately responsible for complying with the relevant planning rules and building regulations. Anyone carrying out development must make a planning application. It is worth noting that some building work may not require planning permission and may be deemed to be 'permitted developments', such as:

- A small extension i.e. a porch
- A garage
- Conversion of a space or cellar space to living accommodation
- A small conservatory

However, you should always contact your local planning authority, prior to the commencement of any building works. The regulation applies to England and Wales; Scotland has its own set of building regulations.

Party Walls Act 1996

The Act came into force on 1 July 1997, and applies throughout England and Wales. (The Act does not apply to Scotland or Northern Ireland). It provides a basis for preventing disputes in relation to party walls, party structures, boundary walls and excavations near neighbouring buildings.

The main types of party walls are:

- A wall that stands on the lands of 2 (or more) owners and forms part of a building - this wall can be part of one building only or separate buildings belonging to different owners
- A wall that stands on the lands of two owners but does not form part of a building, such as a garden wall, but not including timber fences
- A wall that is on one owner's land but is used by two (or more) owners to separate their buildings

Anyone proposing to carry out work (anywhere in England and Wales) of the kinds defined in the 'Party Wall Act' must give adjoining owners/neighbours notice of their intentions.

Note: the act is separate from obtaining planning permission or building regulations approval.

Landlords may have to rely on a tenant to pass this type of notice on to them, as it may arrive as a notice put through the rental door. So it may be practical for the landlord to insert a clause in the tenancy contract stating the following:

"Tenants should make the landlord aware of any notices they receive regarding the Party Wall Act".

Setting Rent and Rent Period

The amount of rent and the date the rent is paid should be set out in the tenancy contract. However, sometimes the tenant may need to change the date they pay the rent. Most times this could be due to the tenant changing jobs and their salary is being paid on a different date. This can be handled in one of two ways:

1. Give the tenant a new tenancy contract or amend the existing contract to incorporate the new date and ask the tenant for the extra payments to make up the days.

2. Continue with the tenancy but agree that the rent can be paid a week later. There is no law that states rent has to be paid a month in advance. The default position is that rent is due in arrears. So if a landlord agrees for the tenant to pay the rent a bit later, it will still be payable in advance but just not the whole month.

With option 2 this can be done either by agreement or (if preferred) on a new tenancy agreement or an amendment attached to the original agreement. Always ensure both you and the tenant sign the new agreement and the new date is kept on record.

Section 1 Recap

What is a Safe Agent:

a) An organisation that protects clients' money
b) Redress organisation
c) Alternative dispute organisation
d) Deposit protection scheme

What could happen if a Landlord failed to gain permission from their mortgage lender to rent out their property:

a) Insurance policies could be invalid
b) The landlord could be ordered to repay the loan
c) A black mark may be put against the landlord's credit rating
d) All of the above

What would be classed as one of the main types of the 'Party Wall Act:

a) A wall that is on one owner's land but is used by two (or more) owners to separate their buildings
b) Planning permission to erect a fence
c) All types of building work
d) Specific building work undertaken at a property

Answers at the back of the book.

SECTION 2

Setting up a Tenancy

Cleaning and Preparing the Property

It can be difficult for a landlord to detach themselves from their property, in particular, if it's a landlord's first investment. Preparing a property for rent is very different to preparing a property you are going to live in yourself. Your selection of decoration and furniture can be very personal to you and may not be a suitable choice for your tenants. Keeping the décor and colour throughout the property as neutral as possible will be more appealing to the tenant and will feel less personal to you. Keep your choices simple and as clean and efficient as possible!

Before placing the property on the market, time should be taken to clean the property and this should be done to a professional standard. Some landlords prefer to clean the property themselves whilst others prefer to use a professional cleaner or cleaning company. In any case, it is important to remember that if an item is not clean at the beginning of the tenancy, the tenant cannot be expected to be charged for cleaning it when the tenancy ends.

It is at the cleaning stage when items that require attention or repair can be noted and dealt with. Although it may appear an unnecessary expense to replace older appliances, it may well incur less hassle and be less expensive to do so in the long run. If you have any items of sentimental or financial value it may be more practical to remove these items and place them in storage.

Most landlords will rent a property unfurnished for the following reasons:

- Furnished properties often don't command more rental income

- Furniture will have to meet the fire and safety legal requirements
- The majority of tenants prefer to bring their own furniture

Although most rental properties will be unfurnished, most landlords will provide 'white goods' such as cooker, fridge and washing machine.

Landlord's Record Keeping

It is paramount that landlords keep clear records of transactions including conversations, emails and phone messages with their tenants and agent. If the tenant complains about repairs to the property, it would be difficult for the landlord to prove that the issues were dealt with if there is no record. It would also be a good idea to obtain a dated signature from the tenant to confirm that the repairs or any other complaints have been dealt with.

Advertising for Tenants

There are a number of ways to advertise a property, none of which will break the bank:

- Advertise in your local paper
- Place a postcard in the local newsagent's window
- Do it yourself 'To Let' boards – boards can be purchased online. More properties are let through 'To Let' boards than any other form of advertising. There is nothing stopping a landlord from placing their own board outside their property (unless they live in an area where this is not allowed). More information about 'To Let' boards, sizes of boards etc. can be found on the 'Town and Country' planning web site
- Spread the word with neighbours, work colleagues and friends
- A number of companies will allow landlords to advertise on all major property portals such as Rightmove, Prime Location and others

Letting Agent or DIY

There are many good reasons for choosing a letting agent to manage a rental property, for example: a landlord may not have the time to manage the property themselves or they may live at a distance from the property. Whether a landlord is considering managing their own rental property or employing an agent, in either case he/she should acquire the necessary skills. As mentioned earlier, in a previous chapter, knowing your rights and responsibilities is the first step in protecting yourself and your investment. By all means employ an agent but ensure you yourself have a good idea of what to do and how to instruct the agent should anything go wrong.

How to Choose a Good Letting Agent

There are many good High Street agents but unfortunately there are just as many bad ones. Many landlords do not take the time to perform checks on a letting agent and generally they are the ones who come unstuck when things start to go wrong. By all means employ an agent if you feel this is the way you want to go, but make sure you do the checks!

The following ten Top Tips will help you make some well-considered decisions:

1. Ask for recommendations
2. What experience/qualifications does the agent have
3. Ensure the agent is a member of one of the organisations listed in this book
   o Client Money Protection (CMP)
   o Re-dress scheme
4. Discuss what you want the agent to do
5. How much involvement you will have
6. The deposit scheme used to protect the tenants' deposit
7. Who will take care of repairs and maintenance to the property
8. The agents' fees and their business terms and conditions
9. What involvement the agent will have in respect of emergencies
10. When you have found the right agent, always keep a record of any correspondence between you, the agent and the tenant

Energy Performance Certificates (EPC)

From the 1st October 2008, all properties for rent and for sale in England, Wales and Scotland will be required by law to have an Energy Performance Certificate (EPC). An Energy Performance Certificate is the key to how energy efficient a home is on a scale of A-G. The most efficient homes being an A and the least efficient being a G.

Band A should have the lowest fuel bills. The certificate also states on a scale of A-G, the energy impact the home has on the environment. The average property in the UK will be within bands D-E for both ratings. The certificate also includes ways to improve the energy efficiency, help save money and also help the environment.

The landlord or letting agent will have to show the EPC to potential tenants before they move into the property. A tenant cannot legally move into a property until an Energy Performance Certificate has been produced. Failure to do so could result in the landlord being unable to rely on a Section 21 (notice to quit). (More about this later).

EPC certificates are valid for 10 years.

Note: There will be no need for EPC's for current tenancies or renewals to the same tenants.

How to Obtain an Energy Performance Certificate

EPC's are performed by a Domestic Energy Assessor (DEA). Details can be found in your local paper, internet or via one of the 'Landlords Associations'.

From April 2018, it will be illegal to rent out a property with an F or G energy performance certificate rating under a new tenancy contract. From April 2016, tenants residing in properties currently rated F or G will be able to request energy improvements to a property. A landlord will not be able to refuse a tenant's 'reasonable request' for energy efficiency improvements.

From April 2018, the proposed legislative changes would make it unlawful to let residential or commercial properties with an EPC Rating of F or G (i.e. the lowest 2 grades of energy efficiency). By April 2020, the minimum requirement of an E or above rated property will apply to both new and existing lets. By 2025 all rental properties will have to have a rating of D or above. By 2030, the government have set the target that all rental properties have to be at least a **C** energy efficiency rating.

Making sure a rental property is as efficient as possible should still be a matter of priority.

How to improve an EPC Rating

- When replacing your boiler, switch to a high efficiency boiler
- Fit double glazing, if possible
- Insulate your hot water tank
- Ensure that lofts and wall cavities are insulated
- Fit seals to external doors to help keep the chill out
- Fill gaps in floorboards and skirting boards

- Replace appliances with those that carry the Energy Saving Recommended logo
- Use energy saving light bulbs

Gas Safety: (Installation & use) Regulations 1998

The gas safety regulation is the most serious of legislation relating to the safety of rented property. In recent years, many deaths have been caused by faulty flues on gas appliances.

What Landlords Must Do

Landlords must ensure maintenance of all gas fittings; this includes gas heating boilers, gas boilers, water heaters, gas coal and log fires, gas hobs, gas ovens and pipe work in their tenanted properties. Landlords must also ensure that they employ a qualified registered gas safety installer to carry out inspections and repairs. Each appliance must be checked for safety within twelve months of installation and at intervals of twelve months of the first safety check.

A 'Gas Safety' registered certificate will have to be given to all tenants when they move into the property and within twenty-eight days of the yearly gas safety inspection.

It is a criminal offence not to comply with the gas safety legislation. Failure to comply with the legislation could result in penalties of up to six months imprisonment and a fine of up to £5,000. However, if a tenant was seriously injured through neglect or failure to maintain gas appliances, then this would be a more serious offence.

Gas safety records must be kept for two years by the landlord or letting agent from the date of each safety check, including:

- Name and address of the Landlord or Management Agent
- Address and date of premises inspected
- Name and signature of person carrying out inspection
- Inspectors or their employer's Gas Safety registered number
- Description and location of each appliance
- Nature of any defect discovered, the remedial actions taken and the date it was repaired

Electrical Appliances

It's the landlords duty and responsibility to ensure all electrical appliances are safe and in working order. By law, (England and Wales) you must ensure that electrical installations and wiring are maintained in a safe condition on all electrical equipment

You must ensure;

- The electrical system (e.g. sockets and light fittings) are safe
- All appliances supplied (e.g. cookers, kettles) are safe

It is advisable to carry out a portable appliance test (PAT) for all electrical appliances. Any plug on an electrical appliance must be an approved type conforming to BS1363. The plug must have a correct fused rating for the appliance to which it is connected. Mains appliances must be supplied and fitted with an appropriate fixed and fitted plug.

Sockets must be safe; it is advisable for a landlord to use a competent qualified electrician to carry out all inspections on electrical equipment. Some gas service companies also offer electrical checks when they perform the annual gas checks.

Note: If a tenant brings a gas or electrical appliance into the property without the landlord's consent, then it is not the landlord's responsibility to have the appliance safety-checked. However, it would be best to discourage tenants from doing so.

Safety Instructions

Tenants should be shown how to operate all appliances left in the property and left with the necessary safety instructions or procedures. Regular checks on the equipment should be performed by the landlord and records of any equipment checked should be shown to the tenant and kept on file for future reference.

Smoke Alarms

Properties built since 1992 must be fitted with mains-powered, inter-linked smoke detectors/alarms but landlords would be advised to provide at least battery operated alarms in older properties.

There is also a legal requirement for 'Houses in Multiple Occupation' to have a mains wired alarms fitted.

Carbon monoxide alarms should be installed in a room where there's solid fuel burning appliances i.e. log burners and open fires. It is also recommended to have a carbon monoxide alarm in a room where gas boilers are located.

Note: It would be advisable to insert a clause in the tenancy contract to make tenants responsible for testing batteries in any smoke alarms. This will give the landlord peace of mind knowing alarms are always operational. It's better to be safe than sorry! Those who fail to install the necessary smoke and carbon monoxide alarms could face sanctions of up to a £5,000 civil penalty.

Carbon Monoxide

Carbon Monoxide is a poisonous gas that you can't see, hear smell or taste – it's known as the 'silent killer' because it can kill before you even know it. When carbon monoxide is released through faulty appliances, low-exposure to the gas can cause long-term damage. High levels of exposure can be fatal. Carbon monoxide alarms are relatively inexpensive and well worth installing in the property for your own peace of mind.

Legionella

Health and safety legislation requires that landlords carry out risk assessments for the legionella bacteria that can cause legionnaires disease, and thereafter maintain control measures to minimise the risk. Most rented properties will be low risk but it is important that risk assessments are carried out.

Simple control measures can help control the risk of exposure to legionella such as;

- Flushing out the water tank system prior to letting the property
- Avoiding debris getting into the system (e.g. ensure the cold water tanks, where fitted, have a tight fitting lid)
- Setting control parameters (e.g. setting the temperature of the calorifier to ensure water is stored at 60°C)
- Ensure any redundant pipework identified is removed

Tenants should be advised of any control measures put in place that should be maintained e.g. not to adjust the temperature setting of the calorifier, to regularly clean showerheads. To inform the landlord if the hot water is not heating properly or if there appears to be problems with the system. The landlord can then take the appropriate action to rectify it. If the landlord is finding it difficult gaining access to the property, appropriate checks can be made to the water system when undertaking mandatory visits such as, gas safety checks etc.

* A calorifier is a sealed tank, which heats water indirectly. Usually in the form of a heated coil which is immersed in the water. Commonly known as a hot water tank.

Asbestos

It is also wise to consider testing for asbestos.

Asbestos is a type of fibrous mineral that is very fire resistant. It was widely used in construction until the late 1980s, when it was discovered to be a serious health risk. When a product which contains asbestos is disturbed, it can release small fibres that are dangerous to inhale. Asbestos can be found in insulation, flooring, pipe lining, and other products. It is important to remember that an asbestos test can reveal low levels of asbestos fibres that could still be a health hazard.

Immigration Checks

Right to Rent

There have been many stories in the news of illegal immigrants entering the UK. To try and combat some of these issues the government have introduced a new law in England. This is referred to as 'The Right to Rent'. It is now become the landlord or agents responsibility to restrict illegal immigrants from accessing the private rented sector. This means that landlords have to conduct necessary checks on all tenants before they move into a property.

Immigration Status

From the 1 February 2016, landlords will need to see, for example, a passport or a biometric residence permit – (biometric permit is an official form of identification provided by the Home Office). In most cases landlords will be able to carry out the checks themselves by asking to see a passport or permit and then photocopying for their own records. If a landlord is, for any reason, in doubt about a tenant's immigration status, they should in the first instance check with the Home office.

Landlords who fail to carry out checks risk a potential penalty of up to £3,000 per tenant. It is advisable for all landlords to look at the Home Office's guidance on unlawful discrimination as well as the 'Code of Practice', which lists a number of acceptable documents to use to verify a tenant's immigration status.

You must do the following:

1. Obtain a tenant's original acceptable documents that allow them to live in the UK
2. Check the documents with the tenant present
3. Copy and keep the copied documents on file and record the date of the check

You should make provisions within the tenancy contract to include the tenant immigration status check. If you ever need to rely on the information you will have it detailed in the tenancy contract.

To comply with the 'Data Protection Act' the tenant should be notified of the information the landlord will be holding on them. They should also be told that the information may need to be submitted to the home office. It is strongly recommended that landlords read the information on the government home office website so they aware of their responsibilities.

Furniture & Fittings (Fire Safety) Regulations 1988, (as Amended 1993)

Although white goods such as cooker, fridge and washing machine are more desirable in a rented property, fully furnished properties do not merit more rent. Most tenants would prefer to bring their own furniture but if a landlord does let a furnished property, by law, they must ensure that any furniture or fittings left in the property comply with the above safety regulations.

The above regulations came into force on the 1st March 1993. All furniture left in a property must comply with the regulations and must have a permanent label clearly showing that certain furniture and fittings are fire resistant. Failure to comply can incur penalties of up to £5,000 and/or six months in imprisonment. The regulations apply to upholstered furniture intended to be used in dwellings. These include:

- Three piece suites, arm chairs and sofas
- Sofa beds, futons and other convertible furniture
- Beds, head-boards, divans, mattresses and bed bases
- Nursery furniture
- Covers for furniture, scatter cushions and seat pads
- Pillows
- Garden furniture that can be used in dwellings
- Any furniture which has been re-upholstered, this includes new and old furniture after 1950

For fire safety reasons furniture which is not fire resistant cannot be left anywhere in the property. This includes outbuildings and attics even if it is just being stored. Furniture and fittings which are excluded are:

- Bedcovers and duvets
- Curtains, carpets and furniture which was made before 1950

If a landlord is in any doubt that any furniture that is left in the property does not comply with the regulations, they should investigate the matter with the manufacturer or the upholsterer of the furniture. They can also contact the Trading Standards Office for help and advice.

Wear & Tear on Furniture

This is where the landlord (at the end of the tenancy) has to apply the fair wear and tear standard to the condition of the items documented on the inventory. These are generally:

- The original age, quality and condition of any item at the beginning of the tenancy
- The reasonable expected usage of an item
- The number and type of occupants in the property
- How long the tenants have occupied the property

The landlord is not entitled to charge the tenants the full cost for having any part of the property or any fixture or fitting put back to the condition it was at the start of the tenancy. This would constitute betterment which would be classed as unfair. Legally a landlord should not end up either financially or materially in a better position than he/she was in at the start of the tenancy.

How to Calculate Fair Wear & Tear

How much the item cost new, how long the item should last for, subtracted from the depreciation value. For example; a chair cost £200, the life expectancy is five years, but requires replacing within two years. This basically means it has to be replaced three years sooner than anticipated. The chair depreciates at the rate of £40 per year (5/200) two years is £80-200=£120. £120 is what the tenant should pay. This formula is classed as fair.

A Sofa was £300 new and expected to last 4 years but only lasted one;

4/300 =£75   Depreciates at £75 a year

75-300 =£225   Subtract £75 from the original price.

The tenant should pay the landlord £225

Furnished residential lettings

Note: As from April 2016, landlords can no longer claim 10% of the net rent as a wear and tear allowance for furniture and equipment landlords provide with a furnished residential letting. Net rent is the rent received, less any costs the landlord pays that a tenant would usually pay, e.g. Council Tax.

Consumer Law

Consumer law works to promote competition for the benefit of consumers, both within and outside the UK. Their aim is to make markets work well for consumers, businesses and the economy. This guidance is aimed at anyone who is managing a rental property, whether they are an agent, an accidental landlord or a landlord with a large property portfolio.

The CMA issued the guidance in response to the 'Advertising Standards' (ASA) ruling. This basically means landlords and agents must make their fees transparent. They should disclose any fees associated with the set-up of the tenancy and make them readily available in their offices, on their website and on any advertising material. The following recommendation guidelines have been put in place to help landlords and agents aware of how they should behave when setting up a new tenancy.

- Advertising and provide information to tenants
- When advertising a property to rent, landlords should be able to answer all reasonable questions asked by potential tenants
- Ensure adverts are clear, accurate and not misleading
- Ensure adverts include sufficient information about fees, costs and charges
- Ensure that any information that can't be included in the advert, due to space restrictions, is easily available elsewhere
- The landlord must have Gas Safety Certificates for all relevant appliances
- Verify any attractive features mentioned in the advertising, parking, views etc.

- Clearly explain what principal features/fittings are included, rather than simply describing the property as fully furnished, unfurnished or partly furnished

During a viewing or any discussions with a potential tenant before they sign the tenancy contract, agents must:

- Treat prospective tenants fairly and give them clear information about any pre-tenancy checks or requirements before arranging a viewing
- Not to conceal any defects or factors which are likely to have an impact on the decision to rent the property from prospective tenants
- Clearly explain what principal fixtures and fittings are included with the letting. If items, such as white goods, belong to the current tenant and will not be included in the letting, this must be disclosed
- Landlords must provide potential tenants and guarantors with clear, accurate and full information to explain what being a guarantor involves. This should include what criteria the guarantor must meet to be considered suitable
- The extent of the guarantor's liability
- The terms of the tenancy contract which the guarantor will be party to
- Whether the guarantor's liability will extend to rent owed or damages caused by other joint tenants
- When drafting or issuing a tenancy contract landlords must ensure that all terms are clear and written in plain language that is easy to understand
- Check that the terms in the contract are fair and that the tenant is not expected to carry out duties which would otherwise be down to the landlord, such as, repairs etc.
- Explain the nature of the contract to prospective tenants before they sign, so they fully understand their rights

and obligations; this should include an explanation of how either party can end the tenancy
- Highlight any terms that are likely to be surprising to the tenant or are unusually onerous
- Provide prospective tenants with a copy of the contract and allow them time to familiarise themselves with the contract before signing it

Property Handover

- During the property handover meeting, the landlord should take a detailed inventory of the property
- Allow the tenant an opportunity to review the inventory and challenge any points of disagreement
- Provide the tenant with a copy of the final, agreed inventory
- Provide the tenant with any important information, such as gas and electricity meter readings
- Provide the tenant with contact details and all legally required paperwork
- Ensure the tenant knows who to contact for help with specific problems in the property

Tenancy Contracts and Licence

A verbal agreement can be made between the landlord and tenant but it is more advisable to have a written contract. A tenancy contract/agreement is a contract between a landlord and a tenant specifying the terms and conditions of the rental period. Tenancy contracts are usually put in place before letting a property. The main difference between a tenancy and a licence is that a tenancy usually gives the tenant a higher level of protection from eviction. A licence for example would be someone (a lodger) living in the landlord's house. Lodgers do not have the same protection from eviction.

Types of Tenancies

There are many types of tenancy contracts that fall outside the Housing Act 1988. Some of the main ones are outlined below:

- Lodgers (Residential Landlords)
- Employees (company lets)
- Agricultural
- Holiday Lets
- Premium Leases
- Rents over £100,000

The above tenancies are not covered by the Housing Act 1988, and would most probably be governed by common law.

If a landlord is in any doubt regarding a tenancy they would be well advised to seek professional advice from a solicitor or from 'Citizens Advice'.

Assured Shorthold Tenancies and Assured Tenancies

There are two main types of property contracts, Assured Shorthold Tenancy (AST) and Assured Tenancy (AT). Certain conditions need to apply for both an AST and an AT to be created. ASTs and ATs are the two most popular tenancy contracts. These tenancies are governed by the Housing Act 1988. This basically means that whatever the law states for these types of tenancies will have to be adhered to. This book concentrates solely on these two types of tenancies.

What is an AST and how does it differ from an AT?

An AST is a written contract/agreement between the landlord and tenant. The written document states what the tenant and landlord agree to do during the term of the contract. For example: the tenant agrees to pay rent for the duration of the contract and the landlord agrees to keep the property in good repair.

The landlord can have as many terms and conditions in the contract as he/she wishes. Also, the contract can be as long/ short as the landlord wishes to make it. However, from a legal point of view the landlord cannot expect to evict the tenant from the property until six months have lapsed (unless both the landlord and tenant are in agreement). Because of the nature of these contracts, there will obviously be more clauses applied to the tenant, but that is not to say that the landlord can include any unreasonable terms in the contract.

An AST does not have to be witnessed (unless it is for a term of three or more years from the outset), in which case it will need to be executed as a deed. A deed has to be witnessed (more about deeds later). Many landlords include unfair terms in a contract without realising it. Landlords should be aware of the consequences that unfair terms can create. If problems arise with the tenant, landlords run the risk of any legal action being postponed if a problem occurred with the tenant's contract which had to be dealt with in a court of law.

Landlords would be well advised to issue a contract that is fair, lawful and written in layman's terms. A tenant must be given time to read and understand the contract and it must not be overly complicated.

The Office of Fair Trading were responsible for protecting consumer interests throughout the UK (one of their responsibilities was related to unfair terms and conditions in contracts). However, the OFT closed on 1 April 2014, delegating their responsibility to a number of different organisations, one of which is Citizens Advice.

The Assured Shorthold Tenancy was introduced by the Housing Act 1988 and amended in 1996. It is the usual form of letting a property if you are a private landlord and your tenant is a private tenant, and if the tenancy began on or after 15th January 1989.

An AST is the default tenancy contract. In essence, this means that if the landlord fails to create a written contract for the tenant (although this is not recommended); at best, by law, the tenancy will fall under an AST. This has not always been the case; prior to the 1996 amendment to the Housing Act of 1988 this type of contract would fall under an AT (Assured Tenancy).

Assured Tenancy

Prior to the 1996 amendment to the Housing Act of 1988 a tenancy was automatically an AT. An Assured Tenancy gives the tenant more protection.

An AT contract is usually issued by housing trusts or housing associations. They offer more security for the tenant and as long as the tenant does not break the terms of the tenancy contract, they may live in the property on a continuous basis.

To create an AT contract a landlord must give the tenant a notice which states that the tenancy is **not** an AST. Ideally, this should be given before the beginning of the tenancy, but notice can also be given after the tenancy has commenced. There is no need to issue a special form for giving this notice; it can be included as a simple declaration in the tenancy contract.

The Housing Act 1988 as amended by the housing act 1996 incorporated some very important changes, one of which was to give the landlord greater protection and make it easier for them to regain their property at the end of a given term. This heightened the appeal of the rental market for investors and consequently produced more rental properties... easing the burden of an ever increasing housing shortage! The AST contract is classed as a 'no fault' contract. This means that a landlord can give a tenant two months' notice (as long as the correct procedure is followed – see later) to quit the property without giving a reason. This notice is called a Section 21.

Joint Tenancy on an AST

A joint tenancy is an agreement whereby a landlord has the option of up to four individuals sharing the same tenancy. (This is set out in section 34 of the Law of Property Act 1925). Any subsequent tenants living in the property can be named in the tenancy contract, but they will not have the same responsibilities as the other four. An example of a joint tenancy can be four friends sharing. All four tenants are equally responsible for adhering to the terms and conditions mentioned in the contract. Basically, this means that if one of the tenants defaults on the rent or damages the property, the other tenants can be held responsible. The following must apply to joint tenancies:

- Each tenant must be 18 years of age or older (16 year olds would have to have a guarantor)
- A single legal document is used to hold the tenancy of all the tenants
- The starting and ending dates for all the tenants must be the same
- All the tenants must exercise equal rights to the whole property
- All tenants must be entitled to possess the entire property with equal rights

There could be a different guarantor for each tenant. This could provide additional security for the landlord.

Replacing a Tenant on a Joint Tenancy Contract

If one of the tenants is replaced by a new tenant on a joint tenancy, instead of creating a new tenancy contract, the landlord could attach a 'deed of variation' to the existing tenancy contract. A deed of variation is an attached amendment to the contract, signed by both the landlord and tenant.

Ending a Joint Tenancy

A landlord must give written notice to every tenant on the joint tenancy and the notice must comply with the tenancy contract with regard to the termination date of the tenancy period.

The following tenancies are ones which cannot be created as an AST or AT:

- The tenancy commenced before the 15th January 1989
- The dwelling is not let as separate accommodation (i.e. the landlord is a resident landlord)
- The dwelling is not the tenant's main or principal home and the rent is more than £100,000 per year. (This level was raised from £25,000 on 1st October 2010)
- A tenancy which is rent free
- A business tenancy or tenancy of licensed premises (where alcohol is sold or consumed)
- An agricultural holding
- A tenancy granted to a student by an educational body such as a college
- A holiday let

All new tenancies are automatically ASTs, whether they are written or verbal.

The landlord has to state in writing that it is to be an AT.

Differences between an Assured Shorthold Tenancy and an Assured Tenancy are:

- If a landlord lets a property on an AST then he/she will be able to regain the property back, as long as the correct procedure and notice is given to the tenant

- If a landlord lets a property on an AT (and this must be done in writing) then the tenant has the right to remain in the property, unless it can be proved to the court that the landlord has grounds for possession. (See 'Grounds for Possession')

Most lettings by private landlords which began before 15 January 1989, are regulated tenancies under the 'Rent Acts'. These are now few and far between.

Regulated Tenancies

A regulated tenancy is a protected tenancy so long as the tenancy contract (which need not be in writing) is still in force. Even if the contract ends on or after 15 January 1989, the regulated tenancy becomes a statutory tenancy and stays one as long as the tenant lives in the property. The landlord can only gain possession of his/her property by proving one or more of the grounds for possession and even then the judge would look at the circumstances and may or may not award the property back to the landlord.

Section 2 Recap

What would be a standard check for an EPC:

a) Internet broadband
b) TV aerial
c) Gaps in the floorboard
d) Sky television

Where do smoke alarms need to be positioned in a property:

a) Each Floor
b) In the kitchen
c) In every room
d) Only where there are wood burning appliances

How would a landlord rate fair wear and tear on furniture left in the property:

a) New for old
b) Tenants must replace any item that shows 'wear and tear'
c) You cannot expect to get compensation for any items of furniture
d) The age, condition and the amount of people in the property

How many tenants are responsible in a joint tenancy:

a) Two
b) Four
c) Five
d) Six

Answers at the back of the book.

SECTION 3

Responsibilities and Liabilities

The Housing Act 1977

The Act applies to regulated tenancies, i.e. all tenancies created before 15 January 1989. Under the 1977 Housing Act, tenants are protected from eviction. Although these types of properties are declining in number, there are still many in operation. Tenants are covered in the three main areas:

- Rent regulation
- Long term security of tenure
- New rules of 'succession' which change what happens to the tenancy after the tenant dies

If a landlord wants to evict a tenant, the grounds for possession are split into 10 mandatory and 10 discretionary. The grounds are set out in Schedule 15 of the Housing Act 1977.

If a tenant dies, the property can be passed to the tenant's spouse, or someone living with the tenant as husband or wife. They will become a Rent Act Statutory tenant, providing he or she was living with the tenant at the time of his or her death. If there is no such person, a member of the tenant's family who has lived with the tenant for at least two years immediately before the death of the tenant will be able to succeed to the tenancy.

Types of Tenancies

The tenancies below are non-housing act 1988 tenancies.

Company Lets:

An AST contract cannot be used for a company let. Company lets are governed by common law (see definition of common law rules) which basically means these types of tenancies are outside the Housing Act 1988. A common law contract can be issued to the company, allowing the tenant (employee) to occupy the premises as a licensee. The company pays the rent. The tenant will have to comply with the terms and conditions within the contract, but the company will be in effect responsible for the tenant. The tenant in this case will be the licensee. (Standard tenancy contracts can be set up for this type of tenancy).

Companies such as local authorities, academic institutes' or large blue chip companies, obviously have the resources to pay the rent and pay it on time. This may not be the case with smaller companies. It is wise to check whether the company is a 'Limited Company'; you can do this by checking on the Companies House website.

Landlords should ensure that the company does not allow a business to be carried out from the premises, as this could constitute a business (commercial) tenancy. A commercial tenancy would give the tenant security of tenure (under the 'Landlord and Tenant Act 1954'). Letting to new start-up companies is risky. It is not unusual for the landlord to ask for guarantees from the directors of the company. (See guarantors). Remember to be safe not sorry!

Rents over £100,000 a year

Now more common and in particular in the London area and the South East of England, these types of lets are outside the Housing Act 1988 and are governed by common law. The rent must solely consist of pure rent. If a cleaner, gardener or maintenance person is employed at the property then the money paid to them can be deducted from the rental value.

Premium Leases

Premium leases are sometimes acceptable to landlords. This is where the tenant pays the whole amount of rent in advance or part of it with subsequent reduced payments each month. Landlords should observe the money laundering issues when accepting premium leases. There may be other implications associated with this type of payment, so tread carefully and obtain advice.

Three year Tenancies

If the fixed term of the AST is to exceed three years, the contract must be drawn up as a deed. The rule here states that it must be clearly noted on the document that it is intended to be a deed. It should be properly executed as a deed. In essence this means that it has to be signed and witnessed by someone who can confirm the signature. It must be delivered by the signatory or someone on their behalf. A standard tenancy contract can be issued but it must be in writing and it must meet the relevant criteria.

Because of the growing interest in creating longer fixed term periods – e.g. three years, the government has produced a model

AST. And, although the new contract can be used for standard AST contracts, it is particularly designed for longer fixed term contracts. It contains provisions relating to rent reviews and others that enable the landlord or the tenant to end the tenancy during the fixed term if their circumstances change. There are guidance notes within the tenancy agreement and it is available from the government website.

Making Changes to a Tenancy Contract

There are many potential reasons why a tenancy contract may require amending. Here are a few of the most common reasons:

- Change in rent amount e.g. rent increase
- Tenant has acquired a pet – new conditions need to be added for pet damage liability
- The tenant wishes to transfer their tenancy to a member of their household who has lived with them for more than one year
- The tenant wishes to change the tenancy to a joint tenancy

It is important to note that any amendment made to a tenancy contract must be in keeping with the Housing Act. Both landlord and tenant have statutory rights which cannot be overwritten in a tenancy contract. If this is the case, the tenancy contract would be invalid, as the 'Housing Act' is the ruling law, which cannot be overruled.

If a landlord is unsure, it is always best to seek legal advice from a solicitor or Citizens Advice.

Clauses included in the Tenancy Contract

- The Landlord must give an address on the contract and this must be in England or Wales. Section 47 of the Landlord and Tenant Act states that demands for rent must contain the address of the landlord. This also applies to overseas landlords.
- Full names should be given on the tenancy contract without titles such as Miss, Mrs etc.
- The full address of the property should be on the tenancy contract; any areas included/excluded from the property such as garage, outbuildings, sheds etc. should be included/excluded in this section.
- Length of tenancy, rent paid and how it is to be paid, monthly or weekly for example. Deposit taken and how the deposit is held: a landlord must let the tenant know where the deposit will be held (see deposits) and how and when the deposit will be paid back to the tenant.
- Forfeiture clause: this term in the contract specifies how the landlord can reclaim the property if the tenant is in breach of any of the terms within the contract. It is important to insert this clause into the contract as the tenant has to be warned about what could happen if any of the terms are breached. Nevertheless, in reality, whatever this clause states the landlord cannot legally get the tenant out of the property without a court order.
- Do not use any of the notices which apply to an 'Assured Shorthold Tenancy' for a Company Let. For a company let, a landlord should also add a clause stating that 'the tenant includes any person derived under the tenancy contract'. A signature on behalf of the tenant would be by a company director or company secretary. It is also important to include in the tenancy contract, how the tenancy could come to an end.

- It is important to choose the right clauses so both the landlord and the tenant are aware of what can and cannot be done within the property and there is no confusion. Remember, the landlord has to be fair and reasonable.
- Where the tenant can go for help and advice such as Citizens Advice, Solicitor etc.
- The tenant has a duty to treat the property in a 'tenant like manner'; this includes checking drains, defrosting the fridge and generally looking after the property as he/she would do if it was their own property.

The landlord is allowed to include any clause in the tenancy contract, as long as it is fair.

The Landlord has a duty of care to the tenant to ensure the tenant(s') safety. The landlord cannot contract out of his/her responsibilities to keep the structure of the property and essential installation services in proper repair. Any clause making the tenant responsible for any of the areas which are the landlord's responsibility will be void.

Guarantors

In some cases the tenant may not be able to provide satisfactory references. This could be due to the fact that they are students, have a low credit rating or they may not have enough money to pay the full rent. A landlord can in this instance accept a guarantor. The guarantor must accept and sign the terms and condition for which they are bound and must be given a copy of the tenancy contract. They should also be given the time to study the implications of the tenancy contract and what is expected from them should the tenant default on the tenancy contract. Some guarantors may be expected to pay the rent arrears and/or any damages caused by the tenant. The terms should be clearly stated on the tenancy contract.

It is crucial to reference check the guarantor as you would a tenant. It is no good having a guarantor for the contract if they cannot meet the requirements and guarantee any financial loss the landlord may suffer. The landlord should ensure they check the guarantor thoroughly, this includes bank, passport and all the normal checks and procedures that the landlord would normally perform on the tenant.

Tenants Deposit Scheme (TDS)
Housing Act 2004

From 6th April 2007, any dilapidation deposit money a landlord receives from a tenant must be placed within an approved scheme. (This won't apply if the landlord has already taken a deposit before this date). The reason for this new law is to encourage good rental practice so both landlord and tenant know their interests are protected. It is therefore important that the landlord pays close attention to the inventory, as this document is a true record of the fixtures and fittings within the property and is signed by the tenant. The more detailed the inventory the more secure the landlord will feel if any damage is done during the course of the tenancy.

The three schemes are TDS, My Deposits and the Deposit Protection Scheme. My Deposits features two schemes, the insurance and custodial scheme. The insurance based scheme is specifically designed to enable landlords to hold deposits themselves. The custodial scheme requires the landlord to hand over the deposit to the scheme administrator.

Both schemes feature ADP (Alternative Dispute Procedures) that can be called on to settle disputes. If there is a dispute over the return of the deposit then it will be passed onto an alternative dispute resolution service. This is an independent person who will decide if the money should be returned to the tenant. A landlord must protect the tenant's deposit within thirty days of receiving it, and they are legally obliged to let the tenant know which scheme they have chosen to use. The landlord should give the tenant a receipt for any deposit paid and keep a copy for their own records. They are also legally responsible to supply the tenant with the Deposit Protection Custodial Scheme Terms and Conditions found on their website.

If a landlord fails to place the tenant's deposit in one of the approved schemes, they will not be able to use a section 21 notice to quit (detailed later). The tenant will be able to apply to the County Court by filing the appropriate form to order the landlord to pay the deposit into one of the two schemes. The landlord could also be ordered to pay the tenant up to three times the level of the deposit in compensation.

Deposits received before 6th April 2007, for tenancy contracts which started before 6th April 2007, do not need to be safeguarded by a tenancy deposit scheme.

Periodic Tenancies and Deposits

If the tenant decides to remain in the existing rented property beyond the initial fixed term of six months, the way the deposit is treated will depend on how the tenancy continues. For a periodic tenancy i.e. the tenancy continues with no new contract, the TDS (Tenant Deposit Scheme) will not apply as no AST (Assured Shorthold Tenancy) will have been created. For a replacement/renewal tenancy a TDS will apply. The deposit previously paid under the earlier tenancy is repayable to the tenant at the end of that tenancy, so it should be returned to the tenant.

Alternatively, if the landlord wishes to continue to hold the deposit as security in respect of the new tenancy it must be protected under one of the schemes (as mentioned). The tenancy deposit is payable to cover the landlord in case the property is damaged during the course of the tenancy. It normally amounts to between 4-6 weeks rental value and is payable up front just before the tenants are due to move in. Any damage that is found when the tenant leaves the property will be taken out of the deposit. At the end of the tenancy, the deposit should be returned to the tenant as soon as feasibly possible.

Some companies are now offering tenant guarantee insurance. This is an alternative to taking a deposit from a tenant and it could be more desirable for both tenant and landlord, especially in an area where there are more rental properties than tenants.

Tenants have the advantage of:

- No large upfront deposit, just an insurance premium equivalent to around one week's rent

- Moving into a property more quickly, no need to save or wait for a deposit on a previous property to be released from a deposit scheme

This insurance could put a property at the top of the tenant's list (in particular if the landlord is finding it difficult to rent the property), something definitely worth investigating!

Tenant Referencing

Ask the tenant to complete a tenancy application form. Don't take any chances; always check the tenant's references. Obtain at least two references, preferably from a previous landlord, employer or bank. Always follow up the checking procedure:

- Check that the person is who they say they are
- They can afford the rent
- The have honoured past commitments and in addition the landlord should ask for documentation providing proof of current and previous address
- Check the 'Right to Rent'

Obviously the more information a landlord can collect on the tenancy application form the better, because should the tenant (during the course of the tenancy) stop paying rent or disappear never to be seen again, then the information contained on the form may well prove vital. It could be used to track the tenant and it can also provide evidence for eviction using Ground 17 (see grounds for eviction), if for example, the tenant used false information on the tenancy contract.

To check current and previous addresses, ask to see the last three utility bills, mobile phone bills or bank statements. Recent bank statements can be particularly useful as this will give the landlord an idea of whether the tenant is in credit and whether money i.e. a salary is being paid into their bank account on a regular basis.

Check all references carefully and make calls to verify them. Carry out background checks too. Don't assume any of the references are legitimate as anyone can create a credible company letterhead. Checks for limited companies can be made through Companies House and on the web.

Credit referencing is a must. You will find many good credit reference agencies online (at a reasonable price) that will perform these checks for you.

Unlawful Discrimination

When renting accommodation, a landlord must not discriminate on the grounds of disability, gender reassignment, pregnancy and maternity, race, religion or belief, gender or sexual orientation. If they do, it means that they are probably acting unlawfully. However, a landlord has the right to make a considered decision in regard to whom they let their property to. For example, if a landlord does not think the tenant will be able to fulfil the requirements of the contract then they have every right to refuse the tenant.

Rent Assessment and Increasing the Rent

A landlord cannot increase the rent during a fixed term period (unless both the landlord and tenant are in agreement). The rent cannot be increased more than once in a twelve month period. The rent increase can be agreed verbally between the landlord and tenant or provisions can be made within the contract. If the tenant is not in agreement with the increase and no provision for a rent increase is included in the tenancy contract, then a Section 13 Notice must be issued with the necessary prescribed wording. A Section 13 Notice can be downloaded from the government website. The appropriate notice must be given i.e. one month for a weekly tenancy, one quarter for a quarterly tenancy and six months for a yearly tenancy.

A tenant and landlord can mutually agree a raise in the rent at the start of the tenancy, but legally this cannot take effect until twelve months have lapsed. The tenant may not have any choice in agreeing with the rental increase as the landlord has the option of issuing a Section 21 Notice to the tenant (without reason) to quit the property. The landlord is then free to find new tenants who will agree to the increased rent.

Rent Review

If the tenancy contract stipulates a rent increase then the tenant has already been made aware that this will take effect. However, if the tenant is unhappy with the increase they have an option to challenge it. They can contact the rent assessment office via the local council. This has to be done immediately. If the tenant pays the increase, then it will be rendered too late and the view will be taken that the tenant agreed to the increase.

If a tenant feels they are paying too much rent they can appeal within the first six months from the commencement of the tenancy. The tenant cannot make an appeal once the tenancy has been renewed or when more than six months have elapsed in an initial fixed term.

Rent Assessment Committees

Rent Assessment Committees are made up of two to three people; usually a lawyer, a property valuer and a lay person, appointed by government ministers. Rent reviews are put into place to adjust a tenant's rent to the current market level. Similarly, the revaluation of rating assessments adjusts the rates paid by an occupier, bringing it into line with rental values.

The assessment briefing covers:

- The rent review terms in your lease
- How to negotiate a low open market rent valuation
- How to appeal against a rent review
- Rating assessments, and how to query your valuation

Note: If a tenant pays the rent on a weekly basis, then by law, they are entitled to be issued with a rent book.

Inventory

A property inventory is the catalogue of a rental property and all its contents. The 'Schedule of Condition' is a record of the condition of all these items. Usually the property inventory and schedule of condition are combined into a single report and can be referred to by either name. An inventory is a record of the condition of the property at the start of a tenancy. It becomes a binding legal contract when signed by both landlord and tenant.

In light of the Tenancy Deposit Scheme (TDS) it is paramount that this document is accurate and thorough. For this reason some agents/landlords employ an inventory clerk. A detailed inventory can prevent disputes and confusion over the return of deposits at the end of a tenancy.

It is advisable to prepare an inventory as soon as possible and certainly before a new tenant moves into the property. When the inventory is complete, it should be signed by both the landlord and the tenant. It is at this stage that any disputes regarding furniture and fittings can be discussed and agreed upon. The inventory can be performed during the property handover meeting. The landlord should take a detailed inventory and allow the tenant an opportunity to review it and challenge any points. The tenant should be issued with a copy of the final agreed inventory. A detailed Inventory will most certainly make life easier at the end of the tenancy.

A good inventory is proof of the state of a property at the beginning of the tenancy and the more detailed the inventory, the easier it will be to resolve any potential disputes.

The inventory should list the complete contents of a property. It is also a good idea to take photographs of furniture and fittings and attach these to the inventory. Photographs may not show the true extent of any damage so always date the photograph and ask the tenant to sign the back of it. This is a good back-up to anything which is written down on the inventory.

If the property has a garden then it should be included in the inventory. It is generally down to the tenant to maintain the garden, but sometimes the landlord may want to employ a gardener and incorporate the charges into the rent. This may be advisable if it is a large or high-maintenance garden.

Housing Benefit

If a tenant is on a low wage he/she may be able to claim housing benefit from their local authority. The amount a person can claim is assessed on a number of criteria, such as salary and savings, etc. The procedure is as follows: once the person makes a claim the property will be evaluated by a rent officer who will then assess the rental value in comparison with other properties in the area and whether the property is appropriately priced for the tenant's means.

It can take quite a few weeks before housing benefit is paid, but in order to speed up the process a landlord can ensure all the relevant paperwork is in order and has been completed in full. This includes proof of the tenant being offered the property, and could also include a tenancy contract or rent book etc. A tenant can authorise the housing benefit department to pay the landlord directly.

The landlord could seek payment direct from the housing benefit agency only if the tenant becomes in arrears with the rent (this would have to be around eight weeks rent arrears) and would not need the claimant's consent. However, the landlord should bear in mind that the agreement is between the landlord and the tenant and the responsibility lies with the tenant, rather than the housing benefit department.

The rules on housing benefit are complicated. More information about the calculation of housing benefit payments can be obtained from the local authority housing department.

Universal Credit

Universal Credit is a new type of benefit designed to support people who are on a low income or out of work. It will replace six existing benefits:

1. Income-based Jobseeker's Allowance
2. Income-related Employment and Support Allowance
3. Income Support
4. Child Tax Credit
5. Working Tax Credit
6. Housing Benefit

It is currently being rolled out across the UK. The new system is based on a single monthly payment, transferred directly into a bank account. At present Universal Credit only affects newly unemployed people in certain areas of the country.

Universal Credit is paid in the following ways:

- It will be paid monthly into the person's designated bank account
- If a tenant gets help with their rent, this will be included in the monthly payment – the tenant will pay their landlord directly
- If a person lives with a partner and they are both eligible, they will receive one monthly joint payment
- It can take several weeks after the claim is made to get the first payment

Contrived Letting

You will need to obtain permission from the 'Authorities' if you rent your property to a family member who is claiming 'Local Housing Allowance' (LHA).

Some tenancies are set-up to take advantage of the housing benefit system. This is called a 'contrived tenancy'. For example, if a family member were to let a property to another family member and only asked for rent when the family member was not working (and so eligible for housing benefit) but did not ask for rent when the family member was working (earning too much to claim housing benefit), this would be a contrived tenancy.

It is the landlords' responsibility to comply. If a landlord does not comply he/she could find the authorities clawing back the LHA payments from the landlord that were initially paid to the tenant.

One way of proving that you are not dealing with a contrived let may be to employ a letting agent. The letting agent is impartial and has a vested interest in keeping the tenancy on a professional level. Definitely worth a thought!

Property Handover

The landlord should provide the tenant with any important information, such as gas and electricity meter readings, contact details and all legally required paperwork including contact information regarding any deposits and inventory. It is important to ensure the tenant knows whom to contact for help with specific problems in the property. Before the tenant moves into the property, the landlord should ensure the tenants are issued with following information:

- Details on the gas and electricity supplier (they have the right to change the supplier if they so wish)
- EPC
- Gas Safety Certificate
- Tenant guide 'How to Rent'
- Deposit information
- Inventory
- Where the water stopcock is located
- Emergency telephone numbers
- Keys to the property
- What day the bin is emptied
- How timers or storage heaters work
- The community charge council property number i.e. 'Council Tax Band'
- Instructions for any appliances
- Emergency contact number

Money Laundering

Money laundering is defined as a process whereby criminals attempt to hide the true source of the proceeds of their criminal activities. In other words: money which has been obtained illegally by criminals, who then try and reuse the money through a number of legal transactions. They do this in order to make the money look as though it came from lawful earnings. For example: if a bank robber tried to use the proceeds of their criminal activity as a premium payment on a rental property.

As from 15th December 2007, anyone running a business will need to have knowledge of money laundering issues and certain businesses will have to have a number of procedures in place to comply with the legislation. If customers offer large cash payments in return for goods, it is up to the business owner to decide whether it is suspicious enough to report to the police. In the case of a new business that handles large amounts of money, this business will need to have anti money laundering controls in place and be registered with HMRC (Revenue and Customs) before they start trading.

Note: If you run a business and you accept cash payments over 15,000€ (about £10,000) you could end up in prison if you fail to do the following:

- Get proper ID from your customer
- Register with Customs and Excise prior to accepting the cash
- Report the matter if you are suspicious that the money could be related to a crime

Data Protection

The Data Protection Act gives individuals the right to know what information is held about them. Individuals have a wide range of rights under the Data Protection Act, including access, compensation and the prevention of processing their information.

General Data Protection Regulation (GDPR) came into force May 25 2018. It affects many businesses and how they operate.

The Act has been updated and modernised to meet today's technology and the way personal information is held. The last time data protection was updated was in the nineties and since then we have seen an explosion of technology to include the internet, smart phones etc. People feel they have lost control of how their data is being used and stored, so the GDPR has put in place stricter guidelines on the handling of personal data. There are serious consequences for those who do not comply with the law and if you are ever investigated by the Information Commissioner's Office (ICO) you will have to show that you are meeting all six principals (listed below).

- What is personal data? Personal data is any piece of information such as name, address, date of birth that you can use on its own or with another piece of information to identify a person. If landlords only retain paper records and not online records they may not need to register. Always check with the official website for any updates to this new law. (This can be done on the ICO website)

Landlords will also be required to keep internal audits as follows;

- Ensure you know what personal data you hold on a person
- Send a privacy notice to your tenants with the old adage, what, who, where and why....for example; what, who and why the information is being collected and used, where it is being collected, stored and shared. Ensure the notice is written in layman's terms. No special notice is required - a simple form requiring a signature will suffice. (Keep a signed copy for your records)
- Storing information securely. If storing the information on a digital device, such as a computer, you must be able to show that it is protected with anti-virus software. If the information is contained in a physical file you must ensure that it is securely locked away in a fire-proof environment (such as a filing cabinet)
- Record the safety measures you have taken to ensure the data is safe
- If a tenant asks you to supply a copy of the information you are holding on them, have a process in place to supply this to them, free of charge (you have one month to provide them with the information)
- If you are holding data you need to show the purpose for holding it (don't hold on to data unnecessarily)
- If your tenant asks you to remove their data from your system, you must be being able to demonstrate that this can be done quickly and efficiently

The following six Data Protection principles are the guidelines and as long as you follow these you will be operating within the law.

1. Using the data in a way the person would reasonably expect

- o thinking about the way you use the data and whether or not it would have an adverse effect on the data subject.(the data subject in this case will be your tenant)
- o ensuring the data subject knows how the information would be used by being open and transparent (i.e. through a privacy notice)
- o It must be collected for specified explicit and legitimate purposes. It must not be processed beyond the original purpose for landlords and agents except for statistical purposes

2. Personal data must be adequate, relevant and limited to what is necessary in relation to the purposes for which the data is processed
3. Data processors must ensure the information is accurate and up to date
4. Inaccurate information must be erased or altered
5. It must be stored so that storage is time-limited. This means the data should be kept in a form which allows identification of data subjects no longer than is necessary for the purposes for which the personal data is processed (including collected and stored)
6. Data should be processed in a way which ensures appropriate security for the personal data, including protection against unauthorised processing, accidental loss, destruction or damage

Terms in the Assured Shorthold Tenancy

An Assured Shorthold Tenancy contract could be oral or written; if a verbal agreement was concluded between a landlord and tenant (although this is not advisable) then the law states the agreement will be an 'Assured Shorthold Tenancy'.

The main reason for creating a tenancy contract is to set out the tenant's and landlord's obligations to each other. Having a clear and concise tenancy contract will help prevent problems during the course of the rental period. If it becomes necessary to evict a tenant, the landlord cannot use the 'Accelerated Possession Procedure' unless the tenancy contract is in writing. Once a tenant is in occupation, a landlord cannot force them to sign a contract. It is therefore essential that the contract is signed in advance of the tenant (s) taking up residency in the property.

A contract can be tailor-made to suit the landlord's requirements but it must be fair and just. The contract can be dated after everyone has signed it. The date should be the date the term begins.

As many as four tenants can be named on the tenancy contract; all four tenants are jointly responsible for a proportion of the rent. This means that if one tenant leaves the property, the others are responsible for paying their share of the rent.

Most landlords will offer a six-month fixed term contract. If the landlord decided to let the property for one year (if this was more agreeable to the tenant), then a break clause could be inserted into the contract. A break clause gives the tenant the right to leave the property or the landlord the right to regain the property, after the initial six months (providing the correct notices have been issued). This could be more beneficial to the landlord, in particular if a tenant proved to be unsatisfactory.

Express and Implied Terms in a Contracts

A contract can be either an express contract or an implied contract. An express contract is one in which the terms are expressed verbally, either orally or in writing. An implied contract is one in which some of the terms are not expressed in words.

An Implied Term in a Contract

An implied contract can either be implied in fact or implied in law. A contract which is implied in fact is one in which the circumstances imply that the parties have reached an agreement, even though they have not done so expressly. For example, by employing a gas safety person to check the gas boiler, you agree to pay a fair price for the service. If you refuse to pay after completion of the work, you have breached a contract, implied in fact.

An Express Term in a Contract

An express term is laid down by the parties themselves. An express contract is when the parties discuss the terms and come to an agreement (either verbally or in writing) before money is exchanged and agreed upon. For example: I offer to sell you my car and, after some negotiations, you agree to purchase it on the terms we have worked out verbally.

Sub-let and Assignment

Written permission from the landlord is required to sub-let a rental property or assign a tenancy contract. In the case of a leasehold property, permission should be sought from the freeholder.

Sub-let

A sub-let is when the original tenant allows someone (a sub-tenant) to live in the property and the original tenant accepts rent from the sub-tenant for all or part of the term of the tenancy contract. In this situation, a new tenancy contract (a sublease), must be signed by both the original tenant and the sub-tenant. In effect, the original tenant then becomes the sub-tenant's landlord. Both this relationship and the one with the original landlord involve enforceable rights and responsibilities. The sub-tenant has the same rights and obligations outlined in the original tenancy contract, no more and no less. The contract with the sub-tenant cannot be in contradiction with the original tenancy contract.

Assignment

When the original tenant finds someone to take over the tenancy contract (usually to get out of a fixed-term tenancy early or when transferring ownership) the new tenant assumes all of the rights and responsibilities under the original tenancy contract. An exception to this is when the landlord and new tenant agree to new terms or sign a new contract.

Landlord's Permission

A landlord cannot unreasonably refuse a sub-let or assignment. If the landlord reasonably believes that the person won't be able to adhere to the terms of the tenancy contract, the landlord can refuse the request for an assignment or sublease. Tenants can apply for dispute resolution if they believe their landlord has been unreasonable in refusing to allow a sub-let or assignment.

For assignments, a landlord can collect information and perform a credit check on the proposed tenant. However, the landlord can refuse to allow the assignment if the checks prove to be unsatisfactory. The fees associated with confirming a proposed tenant's suitability cannot be passed on to the original tenant.

If a tenant sub-lets or assigns their tenancy without the landlord's written permission, the landlord can serve notice to end the tenancy. This basically means the tenancy would also end for the sub-tenant unless they're able to negotiate a new tenancy agreement with the landlord.

Section 3 Recap

What checks should a landlord conduct on a guarantor:

    a) Bank account details
    b) The same checks as would be performed on a tenant
    c) Living in the UK
    d) Have enough funds in the bank

What is a 'Tenant Guide':

    a) It is mainly used to help 'Rent Officers' provide valuations for 'Housing Benefit' purposes
    b) It is a leaflet outlining the immigration process
    c) It is a magazine that can be purchased from the government
    d) It is a tenant guide, written by the government and can be downloaded from the government website free of charge

What is classed as 'Express' and 'Implied' terms:

    a) Unfair terms
    b) Forfeit clause
    c) Terms that have to be written into an contract
    d) Terms which can be written or oral

What must a tenant do if they want to sub-let to another person:

    a) Let the person move in and do nothing
    b) Ask the landlord's permission

c) Pay more rent
d) Ask the neighbours if they object

Answers at the back of the book.

SECTION 4

During a Tenancy

Repairs and Maintenance

Tenants have the right to have their home kept in a reasonable state of repair. However, the tenant still has a duty to look after the property.

By law, a landlord is expected to keep a property in good working order and to undertake repairs to the structure and exterior of the property. A tenant is required to maintain the property and not to neglect the property or to allow it to fall into a poor condition.

Many problems can easily be avoided if:

- The letting contract specifies all the issues in detail
- The tenant is able to easily contact the landlord (or his/ her agent) when necessary, particularly in emergencies
- The tenant notifies the landlord of defects in a timely manner
- Both parties keep dated written evidence of all communications, even when initially conducted by telephone
- Both parties fully understand their obligations
- Landlords/agents respond quickly, especially for emergency repairs
- Tenants appreciate that landlord/agents cannot always get tradesmen to come quickly, especially if the situation is non-urgent

The landlord should be prepared to attend to repairs quickly and efficiently, in particular if the situation is causing problems for the tenant. It is advisable to maintain appliances and check them at reasonable intervals to ensure they are in working order.

Keeping on top of repairs and maintenance will save time and money in the long run.

When undertaking any repairs to the property landlords must be aware of the following:

- A contract is a contract of service
- A contractor-client contract is a contract for services

In each of these types of contract, both parties have specific rights and responsibilities, which differ according to the type of contract in place.

In the case of a contract for a job undertaken by a self-employed person, whilst he or she may hire others to carry out (or help with) the work, he or she is solely responsible for the satisfactory completion of the job.

Houses in Multiple Occupation (HMO) Housing Act 2004

The Housing Act 2004 is an Act of Parliament of the United Kingdom. It introduced 'Home Information Packs', which have since been abolished. It also significantly extended the regulation of houses in multiple occupation by requiring some HMOs to be licensed by local authorities.

If a landlord lets a property to at least three tenants who are not related and the property is not self-contained, then it would most probably be classed as a 'House in Multiple Occupation'. In essence this means a licence may be required.

National mandatory licensing currently only applies to properties that are three or more storeys tall.

An HMO could be described as a landlord who lets out a large property and takes the tenants as individual lets. For example, tenants have their own room but share facilities such as kitchen and bathroom. Tenants can be renewed periodically but it does not affect the other tenants in the property because they do not live communally in the way a family would. Students would most certainly come under this category.

A building would be classed as an HMO if, for example, a property was converted entirely into self-contained flats, and the conversion did not meet the standards of the 1991 building regulations, and one-third of the flats are let on short-term tenancies.

In order to be an HMO the property must be used as the tenant(s) only or main residence and it should be used solely or mainly to house tenants. Properties let to students would be for example, classed as their main residence.

A local housing authority will grant a licence for a property if it is satisfied that it is reasonably suitable to accommodate a given number of people, or if it is made suitable to accommodate the conditions set out by the local authority. The property will need to meet the minimum standards in terms of the number of bathrooms, toilets, cooking facilities etc. The local housing authority will also need to be satisfied that the house will be managed by someone who is 'capable and fit' to manage the property.

Whilst there are many good landlords in the private sector, there are many cases of HMOs being badly managed and in poor condition. For this reason licensing was introduced in 2006 to replace previous HMO registration schemes. It is aimed at producing better qualify living conditions in keeping with the standards required by the licensing laws.

The requirements of the Housing Act 2004 in respect of HMO licensing are dealt with by local housing authorities.

Licence Types for HMOs

The Housing Act 2004, introduced three different types of licensing, two of which specifically relate to HMOs:

- Mandatory HMO licensing
- Additional HMO licensing
- Selective licensing of all privately rented housing in specific areas

Local councils have discretion to introduce additional licensing of other types of HMOs that are not subject to mandatory licensing. This includes poorly converted self-contained flats (also known as Section 257 HMOs, after the section in the Act which defines them). This may be in a defined geographical area or across the whole of a council's area. These schemes are aimed at dealing with situations that cannot be improved in any other way. The council has to consult local landlords before introducing additional licensing and they have to publicise it when it comes into force.

Selective licensing does not specifically relate to 'HMO Schemes' but may be introduced in areas with major anti-social behaviour problems. These problems can have a massive impact in particular areas and to combat these issues selective licensing was put in place to help improve such areas. All privately rented properties within a selective licensing area have to be licensed, regardless of whether or not the property is an HMO. The local council has to consult local landlords before introducing selective licensing in an area, and they have to publicise it when it is made.

Note: An Assured Shorthold Tenancy contract can be used for HMOs.

Note: There are severe penalties for non-registration of such properties, these include a fine of up to £20,000. If in doubt about the type of tenancy issued, the landlord would be well advised to check with their local authority. The other major factor is that if the correct tenancy was not established from the start, the landlord would not be able to invoke Section 21 to recover possession at the end of the tenancy period.

A licence is valid for 5 years.

Note: It is usual and normal practice for a landlord to be responsible for paying council tax on an HMO.

Housing Health and Safety Rating System (HHSRS)

Councils use the following assessment to determine risks on Private Rented properties (PRP).

The Housing Health and Safety Rating System (HHSRS) is a risk-based evaluation tool to help local authorities identify and protect themselves against potential health and safety risks and hazards ensuing from any deficiencies identified in dwellings. This system was introduced under the Housing Act 2004 and applies to residential properties in England and Wales. The HHSRS assesses 29 categories of housing hazard. Each hazard has a weighting which will help determine whether the property is rated as having category 1 (serious) or category 2 (other). Each hazard is assessed separately. The system can deal with 29 hazards relating to;

- Dampness, excess cold/heat
- Pollutants e.g. asbestos, carbon monoxide, lead
- Lack of space, security or lighting, or excessive noise
- Poor hygiene, sanitation, water supply
- Accidents - falls, electric shocks, fires, burns, scalds
- Collisions, explosions, structural collapse

The HHSRS 29 Categories

Physiological
1. Damp & Mould Growth
2. Excess Cold
3. Excess Heat
4. Asbestos (& MMF)
5. Biocides
6. Carbon Monoxides etc.
7. Lead
8. Radiation
9. Uncombusted Fuel Gas
10. Volatile Organic Compounds

Physiological

11. Crowding & Spacing
12. Entry by Intruder
13. Lightning
14. Noise

Infection

15. Domestic Hygiene etc.
16. Food Safety
17. Personal Hygiene
18. Water Supply Biocides

Safety
19. Falls in bath etc.
20. Falls on levels etc.
21. Falls on stairs or steps
22. Falls between levels
23. Electrical Hazards
24. Fire
25. Hot Surfaces
26. Collision/Entrapment
27. Explosions
28. Position and Operability of Amenities
29. Structural Collapse

Routine Visits for Maintenance and Right of Refusal

The landlord has a right to reasonable access to inspect the property and also to carry out repairs. What 'reasonable access' means depends on why the landlord needs to gain access. For example, where the emergency is deemed to cause immediate injury to people or major damage to property then the landlord is entitled to immediate access to carry out any necessary repair work.

The landlord also has a right to enter the property to inspect the state of repair, but they should always ask for the tenant's permission and should give notice of between 24 and 48 hours at least.

The contract the landlord draws up with the tenant should allow access for any repair, maintenance or safety checks to be carried out. The landlord will have to take 'all reasonable steps' to ensure this work is carried out. This may include giving written notice to a tenant with a request for access and an explanation of the reason. The landlord should keep a record of any action, in case a tenant refuses access and the landlord needs to demonstrate the steps taken.

As an example, it is important that the boiler is checked every year. If a tenant continually refuses entry to the property the landlord may have to take steps to contact the 'Health and Safety Executive' (HSE).

If the tenant is a lodger and a landlord provides a service to clean and maintain their room, in this instance the landlord has the right to enter and does not need permission. The landlord does not have an automatic right to enter in any other circumstances unless he/she has been issued with a court order.

Landlord/Tenant Relations

The best way of achieving a good relationship with tenants is by following management practices that are fair and reasonable. It is important to try and maintain a positive relationship with tenants. In fact, it is in the interest of both tenant and landlord to have an agreeable relationship. The landlord wants the property to be looked after and for the rent to be paid on time. The tenants want to be able to get on with their lives without constant interference from the landlord. Unfortunately, for whatever reason, relationships break down and things may turn difficult and awkward.

Communication is the best way to keep the relationship on track. Tenants should have a telephone number where they can reach the landlord. If a landlord is not returning the tenant's calls, he/she will not be aware of any problems that arise and the tenant will a) be less likely to contact the landlord in future and b) get angry and frustrated...And this is how relationships break down.

If a landlord needs to visit the property, they should give the tenant plenty of notice. Unless it's needed for such things as repairs and emergences, a landlord should only be making visits every few months to inspect the property. Respecting a tenant's privacy is vital to the landlord/tenant relationship. Although tenants will want to know the landlord is available when they need them, the landlord shouldn't be harassing them through visits or phone calls. They should respect the tenant's right to 'quiet enjoyment'.

If something needs fixing in the property, the onus is on the landlord to make arrangements to have it done as quickly as possible. As soon as a landlord has been notified of an issue, this should be dealt with as soon as reasonably possible.

If the tenant has an issue then the landlord should take steps to try and resolve it quickly. The matter might be relatively simple but it is best not to allow issues to escalate. Any problems are best nipped in the bud – and fast!

Harassment

It is an offence for a landlord to do anything which they know is likely to make the tenant leave the property. This could include, for example, repeatedly disturbing the tenant or obstructing access to the property, changing locks or disconnecting supplies of water, gas or electricity.

If a tenant is subjected to harassment, then he/she has the right to report the incidents to the 'Tenancy Relations Officer' of their local authority or to the police.

It is against the law for a landlord to harass a tenant. Harassment can include both actions and language that the tenant finds offensive.

Emergencies

Tenants may experience emergencies in the property and this could occur outside the normal office hours, so it would be practical for the landlord to provide the tenant with the following information:

- An emergency contact number
- Instructions as to how turn off the gas and what to do in the event of a gas emergency (gas safety emergency phone number)
- A tenant should be shown any access to escape routes

It's important to advise tenant(s) of the consequences should they contact the emergency numbers with problems which otherwise could be dealt with the next working day. Call-out charges for tradesmen can be expensive so tenants should be warned that they would be responsible for the cost of any non-emergency callouts.

Rent Arrears

There can be many reasons why a tenant may fall behind with the rent. It is important to recognise the warning signs and act promptly and sensitively.

Some common triggers could be:

- Other tenants have left the property (all tenants are jointly responsible for their proportion of the rent)
- They have been made redundant from their jobs
- Tenant may be making a 'counter claim' for disrepair

Often when tenants stop paying the rent, landlords have no idea what to do. So they do nothing! However, leaving the situation 'as is' in the hope that it will 'go away' is not the best way to deal with any situation, as more often than as not it only gets worse.

Sometimes the only way to deal with non-payment of rent is to catch it right at the start. This requires checking that the rent money has been processed by the bank on the date it is due. If it is late by only a few days, the landlord would have a better chance of resolving the situation. Staying on top of the situation is better than ignoring it. Tenants with limited funds are going to pay the creditor who shouts loudest. It all boils down to human nature. If you do nothing, then you will probably get nothing!

Repossession proceedings can be very expensive so the landlord may want to look at other forms of recovery first. But that is not to say that court proceedings should be put on the back burner. Exploring every option can save the landlord time and money. Arrears may be pursued by letters, phone calls or visits, however the landlord should be cautious and not do anything that can be classed as harassment to the tenant. The main options available, other than or alongside possession proceedings are court related options. A landlord can bring a claim to a small claims court for a county court judgement (often referred to as a CCJ) for the rent arrears.

If the tenant contests the claim, the landlord will generally need to complete a lengthy form, called an allocation form. The case will be assigned to the appropriate court procedure, for claims with a value of less than £5,000 it will be normally be the 'small claims track'. When doing this, the judge will consider this form and make directions for this case to be heard.

This however is often futile - if the tenant is genuinely unable to pay the rent they will also be unable to pay a judgement debt. However, many tenants will make a greater effort to pay if they think the landlord is going to apply for a CCJ as the registration of a CCJ against their name will affect their credit rating.

Nuisance and Anti-Social Behaviour

Local authorities receive many complaints regarding noise and nuisance on premises. Noise may be caused by tenants or their visitors and may result in stress being caused to the neighbours and the surrounding neighbourhood. It is a criminal offence for people to cause noise and nuisance. However, the local authorities are able to take action against people causing these problems.

Statutory nuisance can be caused by:

- A high volume of noise, perhaps through parties, music, radios etc.
- Loud sounds emitted from equipment, motor vehicles or machinery
- Rubbish being dumped, which is attracting vermin and pests
- Toxic fumes being released from a property such as gas, smoke or other odours e.g. bonfire nuisance
- Noisy dogs or other types of pets

Dealing with Complaints from Residents/ Tenants

The first step in dealing with a problem is communication and negotiation. Talk to the person causing the problem. Explain how their behaviour is affecting other people. Try to reach a compromise. Do this as early as possible before the problem gets worse. It may be helpful to include a mediator in any discussion.

Note: Landlords should include a noise clause in their tenancy contracts such as "tenants agree not to make noise or nuisance at the property".

Succession and Right of Survivor

If a tenant dies and is in a joint tenancy, then the other joint tenant(s) have an automatic right to remain in the property (right of survivorship). If the tenant was a sole tenant, the right to succession depends on whether the tenant had a periodic or fixed term tenancy. If there is a fixed term tenancy and the tenancy is still running, the executors will arrange for it to be passed on to whoever is left the tenancy in the will. However, if there is no will then the rules of intestacy will apply. Intestacy rules will look at other family members of the deceased tenant who may have the right to the tenancy.

In the case of a statutory periodic or contractual periodic tenancy, the tenant's husband or wife or a person who lived with the tenant as husband or wife, has the automatic right to succeed to a periodic tenancy, unless the tenant who died acquired the tenancy through a previous succession. Only one succession is allowed on the property.

No one else in the family will have an automatic right to succession (S17 Housing Act 1988).

The landlord has a right to possession under Ground 7. This is applicable if the tenancy was a contractual periodic tenancy or else, if it was or becomes a statutory periodic tenancy and if there is someone living in the property who does not have a right to succeed to the tenancy. However, for this to happen the landlord must start possession proceedings within a year of the death of the original tenant.

In the case of an AST, the landlord has automatic rights to regain the property at the end of any fixed term, even if the tenant had a right to succession. However, the landlord must give the correct notice of two months under Section 21, for possession.

Section 4 Recap

What could be classed as Harassment to the tenant:

a) Threatening to evict tenants
b) Shouting at the tenants
c) Changing the locks
d) All of the above

What must a landlord do before he/she rents out an HMO:

a) Nothing
b) Improve the property
c) Apply for a Licence
d) Contact the building authorities

What should a tenant be given to help with emergencies:

a) Landlord contact number
b) Gas safety emergency number
c) Shown access to escape routes
d) All of the above

How many categories of housing hazard HHSRS are there:

a) 10
b) 20
c) 29
d) 30

Answers at the back of the book.

SECTION 5

Ending a Tenancy

Check-out Notes for Tenants

The following notes are intended to help the landlord prepare for the checkout, so that for all concerned, the experience runs as smoothly as possible. It will also help reduce the risk of misunderstandings, deductions from the deposit and any last-minute problems.

Tenancy checkout: In accordance with the terms of the tenancy contract, the landlord has two main obligations to consider when ending a tenancy:

- The property and contents should be handed back in the same condition as they were at the beginning of the tenancy, but allowing for normal wear and tear. Please note, normal wear and tear does not include damage, or excessive wear and tear

- The rent and bills must be paid up-to-date by the tenant. The landlord should contact the appropriate utilities, water rates, and council tax and arrange for final bills. For gas and electricity it is generally easier to inform the tenants of the final meter reading after the checkout. These readings will be recorded during the checkout

Pre check-out visit for tenants: The landlord should write to the tenant; *"It is our normal practice to carry out a pre-checkout visit to the property, about two weeks before you are due to leave. The purpose of this visit is to assess and discuss any particular areas which require your attention. Once the final checkout has taken place, you will not have access to the property and therefore any work will have to be carried out by contractors at your expense. This pre-checkout visit usually takes 15/20 minutes; we will* *contact you shortly to make an appointment. In the meantime, if you have any queries please do not hesitate to contact me".*

The checkout: *"We will contact you to arrange an appointment date and time for your checkout. This will need to be fixed for a time when you are ready to leave the property and hand back the keys. During the checkout we will check the condition of the whole of the property and contents against the inventory, and record gas and electricity meter readings (as listed on the inventory). It is crucial that you attend the checkout process so we can discuss and agree any areas you may wish to point out".*

The Inventory: *"It is a good idea to start your preparations by examining your copy of the inventory to remind yourself about the contents and condition at the start of the tenancy, and to check for damaged or missing items".*

Mail forwarding: *"You should make arrangements with the Royal Mail".*

Viewings: *"It is possible that we contact you to arrange to show the property to potential tenants. It is a condition of your tenancy contract that you allow us to do so. However, we will give reasonable notice, and attempt to make an appointment at a time to suit you".*

Abandonment

Problems can arise if a tenant has left the property and cannot be contacted. Possessions are left behind and it may appear to the landlord that the tenant has abandoned the property. However, the tenant may have abandoned a property for several reasons. They could be in hospital, in prison or simply have left the country.

Most tenancy contracts specify that a tenant must not leave the property unoccupied for more than two weeks. There are several reasons why it is important to include this clause in the tenancy contract:
a) Unoccupied properties are targets for squatters and vandals.
b) Insurance policies demand that a property is not left unoccupied for long periods. It is unlikely that a policy would be valid if a property were abandoned.

A landlord cannot enter the property without the tenant's permission. However, if a landlord has made every possible effort to find the tenant to no avail and the landlord feels that the property is in an unsafe condition, then he/she may enter without permission. However, the landlord must have very good reasons for doing so and if possible should be accompanied by an independent witness.

Caution should be taken to end the tenancy and the correct procedure should be used. Landlords should never change the locks on a property unless they are completely sure that the tenant has vacated the property. A good indication would be if the tenant has left the keys behind or has stopped paying the rent. Always seek professional advice if you find yourself in this situation as it could end up costing you dearly.

Tenant's Possessions

Tenant's possessions cannot be disposed of without first doing the following;

- Make every effort possible to contact the tenant
- Ensure the tenancy has ended (or the landlord could find themselves in breach of the protection from eviction act 1977)

If the tenant cannot be traced and the goods remain unclaimed for three months, items can be sold and the buyer will have legal title to them. Any proceeds can be used for storage, rental arrears or other costs incurred by any breach under the tenancy. Any money left over will belong to the ex-tenant and it may be claimed by them for up to six years.

If the correct procedure is not followed, landlords could find themselves being sued for breach of contract under civil law. They can also sue for illegal eviction which is currently punishable with a fine of up to £20,000 and a potential prison sentence of up to six months.

Professional advice should be sought.

The New Section 21 (Notice to Quit)

The new Section 21 notice is for use with new AST tenancies after the 1st of October 2015 and all AST tenancies after 1st October 2018. The old section 21 (at the moment) can still be used for tenancies which were created before the above date or a landlord may choose to revert to the new section 21.

A new section 21 notice aims to make the possession claim easier and to reduce errors. Previous claims submitted to the courts by landlords were being rejected because the notice dates were wrong in relation to the tenancy end date. Fixed term and periodic tenancies had different end dates which made the process more complicated.

Prior to the above;

- A Fixed term tenancy was submitted on a section 21(1) (b) (ends after six months)
- A Periodic tenancy was on a section 21 (4) (a) (ends after six clear months on the date the rent is due)

Landlords will be happy to know that the two previous section 21 notices are combined into one single notice to be used for both fixed-term and periodic tenancies. This has ended the need for complicated end-dates which was previously required with periodic tenancies.

Two major areas have changed in the new section 21:

1. The landlord cannot serve a section 21 notice until 4 months into the six-month fixed term.

2. If a tenant makes a complaint to the landlord about repairs to the property (this is referred to as retaliatory eviction) and the landlord fails to reply or takes measures to have the necessary repairs rectified... then, the tenant can complain to the local authority. In this situation the landlord cannot serve the tenant with a section 21 (notice to quit) and will be unable to for a further six months after the tenant has made the complaint. This law came into force to prevent landlords from evicting tenants merely because tenants have complained about vital repair work. The tenant needs to report the repairs to the authorities before the landlord serves a section 21 notice, for the retaliatory eviction to be valid.

A section 21 notice can only be used for regaining possession at the end of an AST.

Claims for Possessions

Under the new regulations, landlords submitting claims for possession cannot use section 21 if they are unable to provide evidence that they have issued the following documents to all tenant(s):

- EPC certificate
- Gas safety certificates
- A current tenancy agreement
- Details of the deposit protection and proof of service of the prescribed information
- Where applicable, details of the tenancy arrangements and a 'How to rent Guide'
- A correctly served section 21 notice with proof of service, and proof that the notice period (two months) on the section 21 has expired

The date the tenant must leave is at least 6 months after commencement of the original tenancy (the one they signed when they first moved in), unless the landlord and tenant both agree on a different date.

Note: if the tenant does not move out of the property after a section 21 notice has been served, the landlord must wait until the notice has expired before repossession action can commence.

Fixed Term Contract

It is normal for landlords to issue tenant(s) a six-month contract on an AST. This contract is otherwise known as a fixed term agreement. However, some landlords will insert a break clause in the contract for a further six months, making this an overall total of twelve months. A twelve-month contract may be preferable to both the landlord and tenant. Inserting a break clause safeguards both parties, as either or both can serve notice after six months to terminate the tenancy.

A landlord must give the tenant two months' notice to vacate the property and this must be served on a section 21 prescribed information form (See section 21 form). If a landlord wants to gain the property back during a fixed term period, a section 8 can be issued, stating the terms breached and laid out in the tenancy agreement.

Periodic (Statutory Tenancies) and Contractual

If the landlord does not renew the AST when the fixed term comes to an end, the tenancy will slip into a 'Periodic Tenancy'. A periodic tenancy, otherwise known as a Statutory Periodic Tenancy, takes effect immediately at the end of the fixed-term tenancy. A Statutory Periodic Tenancy will continue with the same conditions, except now the landlord can serve two months' notice at any time using a section 21. It may be advantageous to both landlord and tenant to let the tenancy slip into a periodic tenancy. It means that both parties are not tied into another fixed term contract.

A tenant must give the landlord one months' notice in writing to end a statutory periodic tenancy.

The notice letter should include:

- Name and address of tenant
- Landlord's name and address
- The date the notice period ends
- A forwarding address so the landlord can send the necessary information on the return of the deposit

The periodic tenancy will normally run from month to month (if the tenants pays rent monthly). Two months' notice is required by the landlord for a monthly periodic tenancy. Three months' notice is due if the rent is paid quarterly, and six months if the rent is paid every six months. There will be a notice period of no less than one month that the tenant should give the landlord, which should terminate at the end of the tenancy period. As an example, under the Housing Act (section 5), if the rent is paid on the 23rd of each month the tenancy period will end on the 22nd of each month. However, the landlord and tenant can come to any arrangement as long as they are both in agreement. However, it is easier to calculate the final months' rent if notice is given on the last day of the rental period.

It will be a 'contractual periodic tenancy' if the fixed term contract states it will become one when the fixed term ends and if there is an agreed amendment of terms signed by the tenant. It is important to note that contractual periodic tenancies only exist if the fixed term tenancy contract specifically provides for them. When this is the case, the tenancy does not actually end but continues on a periodic basis, as set out in the tenancy contract.

If there are any disputes regarding statutory periodic or contractual periodic - statute law would usually overrule contract law.

For contractual periodic tenancies requiring more than two months' notice, possession proceedings will need to be started within four months from expiry of the notice. It is important for landlords to understand that if the notice runs out, without starting court proceedings, it will no longer be current and the landlord would have to re-issue a new notice if they subsequently want to take court action.

Serving Notices to Quit

When a landlord serves notice on a tenant or the tenant serves notice on the landlord, it is advisable to send the notice by recorded delivery or hand-deliver it. This will ensure that both landlord and tenant have received the notice and there is no misunderstanding. It would also be a good idea for the landlord or tenant (whoever is given notice) to ask for a signed declaration to state they have received the notices.

The tenant is not obliged to give notice to leave within a fixed period, although in practice the landlords should, in advance of the expiry of the fixed period of the tenancy, ascertain the tenant's situation and whether the tenancy is to be renewed.

If a tenant wants to vacate the tenancy during a periodic tenancy then they must give the landlord at least one months' notice ending on the last day or the first day of the rental period - whichever date the landlord and tenant agree upon.

Note: If a Section 21 notice was served on the tenant but it was decided later to renew the contract, a new AST would need to be created.

Return of Deposit

Deposits should be returned to the tenant as soon as possible. Most tenants expect the deposit to be returned at the check-out. Therefore, it is advisable to inform the tenant in advance of the procedure. The deposit should be refunded to the tenant as soon as it has been released from the deposit scheme. Where it is necessary to obtain estimates for replacements or remedial works to the property there may be a delay in the deposit being released from the scheme.

Dispute over a Deposit ADR

The tenancy deposit protection (TDP) scheme offers a free ADR (alternative dispute resolution service) if a tenant disagrees with the landlord about how much deposit should be returned.

ADR is an alternative way of resolving disputes, other than by using the traditional route of the courts. It is an evidence-based process, where the outcome is decided by an impartial and qualified adjudicator. It is not a process of mediation, arbitration, or counselling and the parties will never be required to meet with the adjudicator. Nor will the adjudicator visit the property subject to the tenancy contract or dispute. All tenancy deposit protection schemes use the 'adjudication' method to deal with deposit disputes.

The parties in dispute are required to submit their evidence to the adjudicator. They will need to do this within a specified timescale laid down by the individual deposit protection scheme. Tenants should check the processes they are required to follow with a particular scheme. The adjudicator will analyse and consider the evidence and make a binding decision as to how the disputed amount of the deposit should be distributed.

The tenant has no obligation to prove his/her argument because the deposit remains the tenant's until successfully claimed by the landlord. A landlord must prove that there is a valid claim to retain all or part of the deposit. If this cannot be ascertained then the adjudicator must return the disputed amount to the tenant. Partaking in the ADR process requires consent by both landlord and tenant. The deposit protection website outlines the full requirement for disputing deposits.

Tenant's Obligations

During the course of the tenancy the tenant is required to meet certain obligations as stated on the tenancy contract but only if these are fair and reasonable.

The tenant must fulfil his or her obligations and remain in the property for the fixed term of six months. (Unless both parties agree to an earlier date).

Landlord Duties

Landlords are responsible for their tenant's safety and undertake other responsibilities including;

- Allowing the tenant's quiet enjoyment
- Not to harass the tenant in any way
- To undertake any repairs which if not undertaken can become detrimental to the tenant's health or living conditions
- To give the tenant 24-48 hours' written notice when requiring a home inspection
- To fit smoke alarms
- To supply a current Energy Performance Certificate (EPC)
- To give the tenant a 'How to Rent' Guide
- To let the tenant know where the deposit is held and supply them with the written terms taken from the scheme's website
- To supply a Gas Safety Certificate to the tenant before they take up residence in the property and also to supply a gas inspection certificate every 12 months. The tenant must be given the inspection certificate within 28 days of any gas appliance being inspected
- Ensure all furniture and fittings meet fire regulations
- To give the tenant an address in England or Wales where the tenant can serve any notices; this must be given within 21 days should the tenant request it

Accelerated Possession (APP)

Claiming possession of an AST

If a tenant refuses to move out of the property on expiry of the section 21 notice, possession can be sought through the courts. There are two procedures that can be used; the 'Accelerated Possession Procedure' (APP) 'Standard Possession Procedure' (SPP).

The landlord would have to apply for a court order to evict the tenant. The accelerated procedure can be achieved for an AST without the need to attend court. The landlord must be able to produce all the correct paperwork and ensure that the correct notices have been served on the tenant and that these notices have expired. The courts must grant the landlord his property back. The accelerated process can only be used if the landlord requires the tenant to vacate the property and not if they are claiming rent arrears, or any of the grounds listed in the 'Grounds for Possession' (detailed later).

Where the tenant has breached any of the terms in the tenancy contract, one or more of the 17 grounds laid down by the Housing Act 1988, must be used and proved. (Detailed later). To start court proceedings the appropriate form would have to be obtained from the local court. Where a tenant is in arrears and a fixed period is coming to an end, it may be more advisable for the landlord to issue the tenant with two months' notice to end the tenancy, then claim separately for the rent arrears.

'Assured Tenancies' have a higher level of security than 'Assured Shorthold Tenancies', if the landlord wants to gain possession of an 'Assured Tenancy' he/she must prove one of the grounds for possession laid out in schedule 2 of the Housing Act 1988, and then it would have to be at the discretion of the judge.

To gain possession of a rental property is complex if the landlord is to use one of the 17 grounds laid down by the Housing Act 1988 (see later). For example: if the tenant failed to pay or was behind with the rent, the landlord must serve a notice seeking possession in the prescribed form (available from a local court) and the landlord will need to prove the ground on which he/she is citing.

Some of the grounds are mandatory (this means if the ground is proven the court must order the tenant to leave). On the other hand if the ground is discretionary, this means that, even if the landlord can prove the ground, the courts do not have to order the tenant to leave. (See 17 'grounds for possession' later in this section).

Standard Possession Procedure

This service lets you complete the court forms online and see how the claim is progressing. This procedure could take slightly longer.

Grounds for Possession

The Housing Act 1988, as amended by the Housing Act 1996, lays down certain grounds under which a landlord may successfully apply to a court for possession. The grounds for possession fall under one of two categories: mandatory, where the tenant will definitely be ordered to leave, if the landlord can prove breach of contract, or discretionary, where the court can decide one way or the other.

Certain terms of the tenancy contract must make provisions for termination on prior notice grounds. (1-5) of the grounds for mandatory possession. For example; if the landlord thinks that at some stage he/she may require their property back, then a clause can be inserted into the tenancy contract (Ground 1). Doing so will allow the landlord to use that ground, if it becomes necessary.

Mandatory Grounds for Possession

Ground 1: The landlord and spouse occupied the dwelling as their only or principal home at some time, and having given notice of intention to return, now wish to do so. (This could apply to a couple living abroad but are now returning). Prior notice must be given; ensure this clause is inserted into the tenancy contract.

Ground 2: A mortgagee of the property now wishes to gain vacant possession in order to exercise a power of sale. Notice will need to have been given to the tenant. The mortgage must have been taken out before the tenancy began and the tenant warned about this contingency within the tenancy contract (as mentioned earlier). Prior notice must be given.

Ground 3: Applies to premises which within the last 12 months have been subject to holiday lets and have currently been let on a fixed term of up to 8 months. Notice must have been served that the property is to be returned to a holiday let. Prior notice must be given.

Ground 4: The premises belong to an educational institution and are normally let to students. This ground applies where the institution has let for a fixed term of up to 12 months. Prior notice must be given.

Ground 5: This ground applies to properties owned by religious bodies, where, for example, the property was occupied by one of their ministers and is now required for another. Prior notice must be given.

Ground 6: The landlord wishes to redevelop and cannot do so while the tenant occupies the property. This ground cannot be used if the property was bought with an existing tenant or the tenancy follows the rent act 1977 tenancy This ground is similar to one established in commercial leases (Landlord and Tenant Act 1954) where recovery of possession is allowed where a landlord wishes to demolish or substantially reconstruct or redevelop the building.

Note: For ground 6, if the landlord successfully gains possession they must pay the tenant's reasonable removal costs (Housing Act 1988, section 11).

Ground 7: This ground concerns inherited or succession rights to a tenancy. It allows the landlord to claim possession where proceedings are started within one year of the tenant's death (or later if the court allows) irrespective of whether rent was accepted or not. The ground cannot be used against a surviving spouse.

Ground 8: This ground has been changed by the Housing Act 1996 and concerns arrears of rent. Arrears must exceed eight weeks if the rent is paid weekly or fortnightly, two months if paid monthly, one full quarter if paid quarterly or three months if paid yearly. The maximum arrears in each case must exist both at the notice of proceedings and at the hearing itself. The ground must be clearly stated so that the tenant knows what he is responding to.

Discretionary Grounds for Possession

Ground 9: The landlord seeks possession because he has offered the tenant suitable alternative accommodation. The tenancy must be on the same basis, for example if the old one was furnished, the new one must be, and the landlord can be asked to fund removal expenses. If the tenant contests it is often on the basis of what consists a suitable alternative accommodation.

Ground 10: Some arrears are lawfully due when notice is served seeking possession and when court proceedings have commenced.

Ground 11: Covers persistent delays in rent payment. Rent does not have to be in arrears.

Ground 12: This ground covers tenants in breach of their contractual (lease or tenancy) agreement conditions, other than rent payments.

Ground 13: The condition of the property has deteriorated due to damage, neglect or default concerning damage to the tenant's accommodation. This ground also covers the acts of sub-tenants, lodgers, tenants' family or visitors.

Ground 14: The landlord can seek possession where a tenant, sub-tenant, lodger or visitor is causing a nuisance to neighbours or is using the property for illegal or immoral purposes. The ground also covers cases of domestic violence where one partner has left and is unlikely to return.

Ground 15: The landlord's furniture has been damaged due to misuse by the tenant, sub-tenant or lodger or any guest of the tenant.

Ground 16: The tenant was an employee (this is classed as a service tenant) and the tenant has left the employment.

Ground 17: This final ground was introduced by the Housing Act 1996 and covers cases where the tenancy has been created as a result of a false statement knowingly or recklessly made by the tenant or someone acting on his or her behalf.

There is also one other overriding reason for seeking possession and that is where it has clearly been shown that the tenant is no longer using the accommodation as his main or principal home. (In other words he already has a property which he can use for accommodation). It is more likely a judge will allow the landlord to regain his property if the tenants have alternative accommodation available to them.

Tenants with 'Assured Tenancies' enjoy a high level of security. If the landlord wants to regain possession he or she must prove one or more of the grounds for possession laid out in schedule 2 (Discretionary Grounds) of the Housing Act 1988.

It is best to try and resolve issues with the tenant and going to court should be the last resort.

Claims for Rent Arrears

For rent arrears, the most common grounds would be grounds 8, 10 and 11. The landlord could use any one or a combination of all of them.

Grounds and Periods of Notice Required

You must serve notice seeking possession of the property on the tenant before starting court proceedings. You need to give the following periods of notice and you must wait until the notice expires.

- Grounds 3, 4, 8, 10, 11, 12, 13, 15 or 17 – at least two weeks' notice
- Grounds 1, 2, 5, 6, 7, 9 and 16 – at least two months' notice

For Ground 14: A landlord can start proceedings as soon as notice has been served.

Where the tenancy is a Contractual Periodic or Statutory Periodic Tenancy, the notice must end on the last day of a tenancy period.

As mentioned previously grounds 1-5 are subject to prior notice which basically means these can only be used if the landlord has notified the tenants in writing before the tenancy commenced that the landlord always intended to ask for the property back on one of the grounds.

Serving Notices Seeking Possession

Section 8 and section 21 notices can be served together in person or by mail. Courts will accept proof of postage or a recorded delivery as proof of delivery on the day, though it is advisable to allow sufficient time for the notice to arrive.

If served in person, ideally this should be witnessed. Personal service is preferable, with proof of postage being the next option recommended. Sometimes respondents refuse to accept and sign for recorded delivery letters, and this can cause delays. **Note**: There are different notice periods a landlord should give a tenant depending on how the tenancy ends.

Claims for Accelerated Possession (N5b Form)

A landlord can obtain the necessary forms from their local county court covering the area where the property is situated or visit their website where forms may be downloaded directly. To gain possession of the property the landlord will need to complete the form for possession on property N5b form.

A landlord should send or take the completed forms to the county court office in the district where the rental property is located. The landlord must produce a copy of the tenancy contract as well as the notice stating the tenancy would be an 'Assured Shorthold Tenancy', a copy of the Section 21 possession notices and a copy of the form and witness statement for each defendant. The landlord will need to pay a fee before proceedings take place. The courts will send the papers to the tenants allowing them fourteen days to object. The district judge will check the paperwork to ensure it is in order and to ascertain that the tenant has not raised a valid objection. The landlord's case will be allocated a hearing date.

The above procedure can only be used if the landlord is reclaiming his or her property on an 'Assured Shorthold Tenancy', has served the tenant with all of the correct notices and these notices have expired. The landlord cannot use this procedure if they are claiming any of the grounds for possession, rent arrears for example.

The landlord would be well advised to seek legal advice if they find themselves in the position where they need to go to court to regain their property.

Important Note: If the N5b form is not completed correctly the Judge will send it back to the landlord and ask for it to be adjusted. This could delay the process.

If you are in doubt about any aspect of completing the Nb5 form you would be well advised to ask someone experienced in these matters to check the form before sending it to the courts.

Section 5 Recap

What is a periodic tenancy:

a) Usually a period of six months
b) It is the term used when no new tenancy contract has been renewed after the fixed term ends
c) It is a protected tenancy
d) It is an 'Assured Tenancy' contract

How many mandatory and discretionary grounds are there to terminate an AST:

a) 10
b) 17

In order to use the APP what must a landlord have:

a) A copy of the tenancy contract
b) A copy of an EPC and gas safety certificate
c) A copy of all repairs to the property
d) A landlord must have the relevant up-to-date property documentation to be able to present it to the court

What is prior notice:

a) It is a notice to quit the property
b) It is notice of your intentions written into the contract for example; if you know that you may need to gain your property back
c) It is a court proceedings notice
d) It is an Nb5 court form

Answers at the back of the book.

Check before Letting a Property

- Landlord needs approval from Mortgage Company
- Obtain an HMO (Housing in Multiple Occupation) licence (if necessary)
- Arrange appropriate Insurance
- Arrange gas safety certificate (must give a copy of the certificate to each tenant)
- EPC (Energy Performance Certificate) given to each tenant
- Check all electrical equipment is in working order and has the correct plugs etc.
- Carbon Monoxide meters where there is solid fuel burning (log fires etc.)
- Legionella bacteria and asbestos test (low risk but good to check)
- Furniture must comply with fire and safety regulations
- Fit smoke alarms on each floor
- Register with a deposit protection scheme (DPS)
- Check tenants' references
- Check 'Right to Rent' Immigration procedure
- Arrange a moving-in date
- Provide tenant with a 'Tenant Guide' available to download from the government website
- Perform an inventory and check the schedule of contents
- Take meter readings and inform utilities of name changes
- Complete contracts (signatures of all tenants) arrange Guarantor if required
- Set up a bank standing order and inform the bank (decide when the rent should be paid)
- Give each tenant a gas safety certificate
- Give the head tenant the inventory, utility readings, tenant information
- Collect deposit and advanced rent from the tenant

- Protect the deposit within 30 days of receiving the money from the tenant and give the tenant information downloaded from the scheme website

SECTION 6

Forms

Assured Shorthold Tenancy Agreement (AST Example)
UNDER PART 1 OF THE HOUSING ACT 1988 AS AMENDED BY PART III OF THE HOUSING ACT 1996

The Agreement is Between:

The Landlord:	
Landlord's Address:	

AND

Tenant 1 Address:	

Print Name:	Signature:	

Tenant 2 Address:	

Print Name:	Signature:	

Tenant 3 Address:	

Print Name:	Signature:	

Tenant 4 Address:	

Print Name:	Signature:	

All names must be in full including any middle names omit (Mr, Mrs, Ms, and Miss etc.)
Note: Where the agreement consists of more than one person, they will all have joint and several liabilities under this agreement. This basically means that they will each be liable for all sums under this agreement, and not just liable for a proportional part.

Section 1

This agreement is made on: **(insert date, month, and year)**

Between (the "Landlord")

Name: ....

Address: ....

Tel No: ....

And ("Head Tenant")

Name: ....

Address: ....

Tel No: ....

The landlord is legally entitled to grant this aforesaid tenancy and is the owner of the aforesaid residential property as mention in section 2 of this agreement.

(Signed by Landlord)..

Date: ....

Section 2

In consideration of the landlord letting these premises to the tenant.

IT IS HEREBY AGREED BY BOTH PARTIES AS FOLLOWS
The landlord lets and the tenant takes the premises known as:
(insert address of Property)

Hereinafter called the "property" together with any fixtures, fittings, furnishings, specified in the inventory

For the term of: **(insert term)**
Commencing on: **(insert date)**
At the rent of £ **(insert amount)**
per calendar month payable monthly in advance

To: **(insert name)**
The first payment is to be made on: **(insert date)**
and subsequent payments made on: **(insert date)**

(Insert day) of each month by bank standing order.

Two months written notice on a section 21 of the Housing Act 1988 will be served by the landlord to end this tenancy contract. If at the end of the fixed term you have not received notice to quit and want to continue with the tenancy; the tenancy will continue still subject to the terms and conditions of this contract. The contract will continue from month to month from the end of this fixed term period until the landlord gives 2 months' to terminate the contract or a new contract is entered into or this contract is ended by a court order.

The Guarantor: **(insert name)**

I hereby agree to take full responsibility for the tenants as named on the first page of this contract for: full rental payment and any other associated costs which would otherwise be the tenants' responsibility, as in a copy of this contract.

Signed: ....Date: ....

Witnessed by: ....

Date: ....

(Section 2) This contract creates an Assured Shorthold Tenancy within part I chapter II of the Housing Act 1988. This means that when the term expires the landlord can recover possession as set out in section 21 of the Housing Act 1988.

1. The property is only to be used as a residential property. Neither the aforesaid property nor any part of the aforesaid property will be used at any time during the term of this contract by the tenant or any other person for the purpose of carrying out any business ventures, trade of any kind, or for any other purpose than a private home.
2. The landlord agrees to let to the tenant at the aforesaid property as aforesaid in (Section 1)
   The tenant hereby agrees with the landlord as follows:
3. To allow the Landlord or anyone with the landlords written authority to enter the property at a reasonable time of the day to inspect the property's condition and state of repair, providing the landlord has given reasonable notice.
4. If there is a guarantor, the guarantor will ensure the tenant will keep to the obligations in this contract. The guarantor agrees to pay on demand to the landlord any money lawfully due which the tenant is responsible for and has not paid.
5. To pay the aforesaid rent as stated in section 2 of this contract to the landlord on the day and in the method aforesaid without any deductions.
6. Not to alter or add to the property or allow anyone else to do anything at the property which the tenant might reasonably foresee would increase the risk of fire.
7. To give the landlord a copy of any notice delivered to the property with regard to the Party Wall Act 1996 within seven days of receiving it and not to do anything as a result of the notice unless required to do so by the Landlord.
8. The tenant must not change the locks without prior permission from the landlord.
9. The landlord is not responsible for the tenants contents in the property therefore it is advisable for the tenant to obtain contents insurance.
10. At the end of the term to deliver the property to the landlord in the condition it should be if the tenant has performed the

obligations under this contract (with the exception of fair wear and tear).

11. During the last twenty-eight days of the tenancy to allow the landlord or the landlord's agent to enter and view the property with prospective tenants at reasonable times of the day if the landlord has given reasonable prior notice.

12. To pay council tax, water charges, electric, gas, television services, phone rental and calls in respect of the property.

13. Subject to the provisions of this contract apart from the tenant no other person(s) are permitted to live in the property without prior permission from the landlord.

14. No guest of the tenant is permitted to live in the property for more than two consecutive weeks without prior permission from the landlord.

15. A rent review will take place twelve months after the commencement of this tenancy (The date this agreement is signed)

16. To keep the property including the garden in a clutter free state.

17. Regularly test any smoke detectors in the property and replace the batteries when required.

18. Not to keep any pets or animals in or about the property without written permission from the landlord. The landlord will not unreasonably withhold.

19. To keep the garden in good order and cut the grass regularly.

20. To remove all furniture and goods including rubbish belonging to the tenant at the end of the tenancy and leave a forwarding address for the Landlord.

21. Repair any damage that was caused by neglect by the tenant or any person living or visiting the property. This includes broken windows and any damaged fittings.

22. If the property is going to be empty overnight and it is freezing weather conditions you must take all reasonable efforts to avoid the water system freezing such as leaving heating on low.

23. Defrost the fridge when necessary.
24. Not to display any notices on the outside of the property.
25. If you give notice before the end of the fixed period you must pay the landlord cost associated with re-letting the property as well as paying the rent until the property is let.
26. Transfer the tenancy to anyone else without prior permission from the landlord. The landlord will not unreasonably withhold.
27. Keep the drains free from obstruction.
28. The landlord may serve the tenant with a section 21 notice to quit the property four months into the fixed period as specified in (section 2) of this contract.
29. Not to cause nuisance or annoyance to neighbours in any way. You must not play loud music in any way which will annoy the neighbours or be heard outside your home between the hours of 11pm and 7.30am.
30. Not to leave the property unattended for more than 21 days without informing the landlord.
31. To use the property only in a tenant-like manner.
32. You must lock all doors when leaving the property and ensure the property is secure when unattended.
33. You must pay 3.75% above the base lending rate for any rent arrears which falls due from the tenant under this contract.
34. If the rent is outstanding for a period of 14 days the landlord has the right to enter the property and take possession and use section 8 of the grounds for eviction to regain the property. (forfeit clause)
35. To comply with gas safety regulations the tenant must;
    a. Keep ventilators in the property free of any blockage.
    b. Any unusual smell or noise relating to a gas appliance should be reported immediately to the gas board, landlord and the landlord's agent.
36. If the tenant stays on in the property after the fixed period set out in section 2 of this contract the tenancy will continue

from month to month. The periodic tenancy can be ended by the tenant giving the landlord one month written notice.
37. To pay on signing the contract the sum of £ **(insert amount)** which is to be held by **(insert name)** during the tenancy as security against any breach of the tenant's obligations. It is agreed that no interest shall be payable on this deposit.

The landlord to inform the tenant where the deposit is held within 30 days of receiving the monies.

At the end of the tenancy the deposit will be returned to the tenant as soon as reasonably practical and after any reasonable deductions to cover any costs incurred or losses caused by the tenant during the course of this tenancy contract.

The Landlord agrees with the tenant:

1. A Gas Safety engineer will carry out maintenance on all gas appliances every 12 months. The tenant is required to allow entry to the property with reasonable prior notice.
2. To supply the tenant(s) with a copy of gas safety certificate for gas appliances in the property within 28 days of tenants moving into the aforesaid property.
3. If the property is damaged to such an extent that the tenant cannot live in it, the rent will cease to be payable until the property is rebuilt or repaired so that the tenant can live there again unless:
   a. The cause of the damage is something which the tenant did or failed to do as a result of which the landlord's insurance policy relating to the property has become void and the landlord had given the tenant notice of what the policy required.
   b. Any dispute about whether this clause applies must be submitted to arbitration under part 1 or the arbitration act 1996 if both parties agree in writing after the dispute has arisen.
4. Any furniture left in the property is to be fire resistant.
5. To insure the building and any landlord contents which are specified in the inventory.
6. That the tenant(s) have the right to possess and enjoy the property during the tenancy without any interruption from the landlord or any person claiming through or in trust for the landlord But:
   a. This clause does not limit any of the rights under this contract which the tenant has agreed to allow the landlord to exercise;
   b. This clause does not prevent the landlord from taking lawful steps to enforce his rights against the

tenant if the tenant breaks any of the terms of this contract.

The landlord is to keep the following in good repair:

- The roof
- Guttering
- Walls (excluding internal decoration)
- Windows and doors
- Gas
- Electricity
- Heating
- Water and sanitation

Landlord's Address:...**(insert address)**

The landlord notifies the tenant that the tenant may serve notices (including notices in proceedings) on the landlord at the address on this contract.

(This notice is given under section 47 of the Landlord and Tenant act 1987). (The address must be in England or Wales).

The landlord needs a court order to repossess the property. You should consult either a solicitor or Citizens Advice, or a Housing Advice Centre if you need legal help and/or advice understanding this contract.

Company Let Form (Example)

For a Furnished or Unfurnished House or Flat
(Please complete the following)

Landlord: **(insert name)**

Registered Office**:** **(insert office)**

Company Registration number: **(insert number)**

Property: **(insert details)**

For the Term of: **(insert term)**

Commencing on: **(insert date)**

At the Rent of: £ **(insert amount)** per week / month
(delete as required)

Payment in advance of each week / month **(delete as needed)**

A Deposit of £ **(insert amount) is**
payable on signing this Contract

The Property is furnished/unfurnished **(delete as required)**

An Inventory is attached to this contract: yes/no **(delete as required)**

THIS CONTRACT comprises the particulars detailed above and the terms and conditions hereinafter printed whereby the Property is hereby let by the Landlord and taken by the Tenant for the Term of the Rent.

Inventory of Contents (Example)

Note: each photograph should be given a number and entered onto the inventory. Photographs should be signed and dated on the back by both landlord and tenant.

No:	Item	Shortcut Key
	Entrance:	No of Photographs:
	Front Door	
	Walls	
	Flooring	
	Lighting	
	Windows	
	Other	
	Kitchen:	No of Photographs
	Doors	
	Flooring	
	Windows	
	lighting	

Shortcut Keys					
Missing	**M**	Scratched	**S**	Broken	**B**
Good Condition	**G**	Damaged	**D**	Repair Needed	**R**

(Cont)

No:	Item	Shortcut Keys
	Kitchen Cont.:	No of Photographs
	Blinds	
	Cupboard	
	Washing Machine	
	Dishwasher	
	Fridge/ Freezer	
	Crockery	
	Electrical Appliances	
	Lighting	
	Other	
	Dining Room	No of Photographs:
	Door	
	Flooring	
	Windows	
	Walls	
	Blinds/Curtains	
	Cupboards	

Signed by Tenant:		
Signed by Landlord/Agent:		
Gas meter Reading	Inward Check	Outward Check
Elec. meter Reading	Inward Check	Outward Check

SECTION 21 FORM 6 A

Notice seeking possession of a property let on an Assured Shorthold Tenancy (Example)

Housing Act 1988 section 21 (1) AND (4) as amended by section 194 and paragraph 103 of Schedule 11 to the Local Government and Housing act 1989 and section 98 (2) and (3) of the Housing Act 1996

Please write clearly in black ink. Please tick boxes where appropriate.

This form should be used where a no fault possession of accommodation let under an assured shorthold tenancy (AST) is sought under section 21 (1) AND (4) of the Housing Act 1988.

There are certain circumstances in which the law says that you cannot seek possession against your tenant using section 21 of the Housing Act 1988, in which case you should not use this form. These are:

a) During the first four months of the tenancy (but where the tenancy is a replacement tenancy, the four month period is calculated by reference to the start of the original tenancy and not the start of the replacement tenancy – see section 21 (4B) of the Housing Act 1988);

b) Where the landlord has not provided the tenant with an energy performance certificate, gas safety certificate or the Department of Communities and Local Government publication "How to Rent: the checklist for renting in England" (see the Assured Shorthold Tenancy Notices and Prescribed Requirements (England) Regulations 2015);

c) Where the landlord has not complied with the tenancy deposit protection legislation; or
d) Where a property requires a licence but is unlicensed;

Landlords who are unsure about whether they are affected by these provisions should seek specialist advice.

This form must be used for all ASTs created on or after 1 October 2015 except for statutory periodic tenancies which have come into being on or after 1 October 2015 at the end of fixed term ASTs created before 1 October 2015. There is no obligation to use this form in relation to ASTs created prior to 1 October 2015, however it may nevertheless be used for all ASTs.

What to do if this notice is served on you

You should read this notice very carefully. It explains that your landlord has started the process to regain possession of the property referred to in section 2 below.

You are entitled to at least two months' notice before being required to give up possession of the property. However, if your tenancy started on a periodic basis without any initial fixed term a longer notice period may be required depending on how often you are required to pay rent (for example, if you pay rent quarterly, you must be given at least three months' notice, or, if you have a periodic tenancy which is half yearly or annual, you must be given at least six months' notice (which is the maximum)). The date you are required to leave should be shown in section 2 below. After this date the landlord can apply to court for a possession order against you.

Where your tenancy is terminated before the end of a period of your tenancy (e.g. where you pay rent in advance on the first of each month and you are required to give up possession in the middle of the month), you may be entitled to repayment of rent from the landlord under section 21C of the Housing Act 1988.

If you need advice about this notice, and what you should do about it, take it immediately to a citizens advice, a housing advice centre, a law centre or a solicitor.

1. To: Name(s) of tenant(s) (Block Capitals)
    You are required to leave the below address after [

    ]¹.

    If you do not leave, your landlord may apply to the court for an order under section 21(1) or (4) of the Housing Act 1988 requiring you to give up possession.
    Address of premises

2. This notice is valid for six months only from the date of issue unless you have a periodic tenancy under which more than two months' notice is required (see notes accompanying this form) in which case this notice is valid for four months only from the date specified in section 2 above.

3. Name and address of landlord

To be signed and dated by the landlord or their agent (someone acting for them). If there are joint landlords each landlord or the agent should sign unless one signs on behalf of the rest with their agreement.

*Signed Date (DD/MM/YYYY)*_____

¹Landlords should insert a calendar date here. The date should allow sufficient time to ensure that the notice is properly served on the tenant(s). This will depend on the method of service

being used and landlords should check whether the tenancy agreement makes specific provision about service. Where landlords are seeking an order for possession on a periodic tenancy under section 21(4) of the Housing Act 1988, the notice period should also not be shorter than the period of the tenancy (up to a maximum of six months), e.g. where there is a quarterly periodic tenancy, the date should be three months from the date of service.

Please specify whether: ☐ landlord ☐ joint landlords ☐ landlords

Agent *Name(s) of signatory/signatories (Block Capitals)*

_____

_____

_____

Address/Telephone number *of signatory/signatories (Block Capitals)*

_____

_____

_____

Self-Check Questions

1. **How long are you required to keep receipts for tax purposes:**

   a) 6 Years
   b) 2 Years
   c) 4 Years
   d) 10 Years

2. **What is defined as common law:**

   a) It is those laws contained in Acts of Parliament
   b) Common law is effectively all law that has not been enacted by Parliament
   c) It is simply property law
   d) It is laws set out in the books of ancient law

3. **What would be a standard check for an EPC:**

   a) Smoke alarms
   b) Carbon monoxide meters
   c) Double glazing
   d) Internet connection

4. **What is a safe agent:**

   a) An agent who manages a property safely
   b) It is a redress organisation
   c) It is an organisation that protect clients' money
   d) It is an agent who has been assigned to a voluntary organisation

5. Which tenancy has more protection for the tenant:

a) AST
b) AT

6. What happens if a contract is not renewed at the end of a fixed term:

a) The tenant is given one month to sign a new contract
b) The tenant becomes a protected tenant
c) It means the landlord cannot issue a section 21
d) The contract automatically becomes a periodic tenancy

7. How much notice do you have to give a tenant on an AST if they have been living in the property for more than a year:

a) 1 month
b) 2 months
c) 3 months
d) 6 weeks

8. A tenant has just moved into a property but no written contract has been issued. What type of tenancy contract would have been created:

a) The tenant would be protected under the 'Protection from Eviction Act 1977'
b) It automatically becomes an Assured Tenancy
c) It automatically becomes an Assured Shorthold Tenancy
d) The tenant is living in the property under licence

9. What is an NRL1 form

a) National Rental Licence
b) Non Resident Landlord
c) National Rental Landlord
d) Non Rental Landlord

10. What is the Landlord's main responsibility to the tenant:

a) To inspect the property regularly
b) To ensure the tenant gets their deposit back
c) To allow the tenant's 'quiet enjoyment'
d) To ensure all necessary repair work is done immediately

11. What would you do if you were given a large amount of money as rental premium:

a) Require all payments to be made through a bank account
b) Keep records of all transaction
c) Notify the appropriate authorities
d) Nothing

12. The main aim of the Consumer Protection from Unfair Trading Regulations 2008 is to get agents to:

a) Not to make a profit from a tenant
b) Tell the truth about goods, services and prices offered by the agency
c) To ensure tenants are credit checked
d) Provide detailed property information

13. Rooms in a large house are let to students, which regulations do you need to comply with:

a) HMO Licence
b) Building regulations
c) Housing Market Officer
d) Planning regulations

14. A company wishes to rent your property. How would you validate a company status:

a) Check they have a website
b) Check on 'Companies House'
c) Contact the council
d) Contact the inland revenue

15. What is a section 13 form:

a) A Notice to Quit
b) Part of the AST
c) Notice to increase the rent
d) An Inventory form

16. How much time do you have to protect a tenant's deposit:

a) 1 week
b) 2 weeks
c) 4 weeks
d) 30 days

17. How would you handle the tenant's deposit:

a) In a client account
b) In one of the approved schemes
c) In the letting agents scheme
d) In the landlords designate bank account

18. What is APP:

a) Accelerated Possession Procedure
b) Accelerated Prevention Procedure
c) Accelerated Possession Process

19. What would be classed as an 'unfair term' in a contract:

a) To ask the tenants to clean the windows
b) To make the tenants responsible for checking batteries in a smoke alarm
c) To ask the tenants to inform you if they are going on holiday for more than two weeks
d) To request routine visits to inspect the property

20. Does a landlord have to include a name/address on the contract of where he/she can be contacted:

a) Yes
b) No
c) It is entirely up to the landlord
d) No, if they are living overseas

Section 1 Answers A,D,A,
Section 2 Answers C,A,D,B
Section 3 Answers B,D,D,B
Section 4 Answers D,C,D,C
Section 5 Answers B,B,D,B

Answers for full self-check questions

1) a
2) b
3) c
4) c
5) b
6) d
7) b
8) c
9) b
10) d
11) c
12) b
13) a
14) b
15) c
16) d
17) b
18) a
19) a
20) a

Index

Printed in Poland
by Amazon Fulfillment
Poland Sp. z o.o., Wrocław